Study Guide for Hurley's

A CONCISE
INTRODUCTION TO LOGIC

Sixth Edition

Robert W. Burch
Texas A & M University

Wadsworth Publishing Company
I(T)P® An International Thomson Publishing Company

Belmont, CA • Albany, NY • Bonn • Boston • Cincinnati • Detroit • Johannesburg • London • Madrid
Melbourne • Mexico City • New York • Paris • San Francisco • Singapore • Tokyo • Toronto • Washington

Philosophy Editor: Peter Adams
Assistant Editor: Clay Glad
Editorial Assistant: Greg Brueck
Marketing Manager: Lauren Ward
Print Buyer: Stacey Weinberger
Permissions Editor: Peggy Meehan
Cover: Laurie Anderson
Compositor: The Cowans
Printer: Malloy Lithographing, Inc.

Printed in the United States of America
1 2 3 4 5 6 7 8 9 10

For more information, contact Wadsworth Publishing Company, 10 Davis Drive,
Belmont, CA 94002, or electronically at http://www.thomson.com/wadsworth.html

International Thomson Publishing Europe
Berkshire House 168-173
High Holborn
London, SC1V7AA, England

International Thomson Editores
Campos Eliseos 385, Piso 7
Col. Polanco
11560 México D.F. México

Thomas Nelson Australia
102 Dodds Street
South Melbourne 3205
Victoria, Australia

International Thomson Publishing Asia
221 Henderson Road
#05-10 Henderson Building
Singapore 0315

Nelson Canada
1120 Birchmount Road
Scarborough, Ontario
Canada M1K 5G4

International Thomson Publishing Japan
Hirakawacho Kyowa Building, 3F
2-2-1 Hirakawacho
Chiyoda-ku, Tokyo 102, Japan

International Thomson Publishing GmbH
Königswinterer Strasse 418
53227 Bonn, Germany

International Thomson Publishing Southern Africa
Building 18, Constantia Park
240 Old Pretoria Road
Halfway House, 1685 South Africa

ISBN 0-534-50536-8

CONTENTS

PREFACE

This study guide is intended to be used in conjunction with Patrick J. Hurley's *A Concise Introduction to Logic*. In it you will find summary statements of the main points made in the Hurley text. You will also find illustrations of these points, worked examples, and original problems for practice. Each section is closely coordinated with a corresponding section of Hurley's text. You should read a given section of the text thoroughly, then try to work some of the exercises in the text. Then refer to the corresponding section of this study guide. Follow through the worked exercises and examples, and attempt to work out the exercises in the study guide. You may check your comprehension by comparing your solutions with those given at the back of the study guide: Answers to all original exercises are provided.

Introductory logic is a subject learned only by practice. It is a skill more than a body of knowledge, and, like other skills, it must be regularly exercised in order to be acquired and retained. Think of logic as you would tennis or bowling: You may know very well in the abstract what is to be done, and you may understand very well when others do it, but you may still not be able to do it yourself. Doing logic yourself is really the only way to acquire ability in logic. So practice regularly and often; work as many exercises as you can on your own. You will find your ability and your confidence increasing. Don't be surprised if logic is even fun.

Analysis in the restructuring of sentences.

1
BASIC CONCEPTS

1.1 ARGUMENTS, PREMISES, AND CONCLUSIONS

Logic is the science that evaluates arguments. An *argument* is a group of statements, the purport of which is that some of them (the *premises*) should support, imply, provide evidence for, or make reasonable to believe another particular one of them (the *conclusion*). The premises of an argument set forth the reasons for the conclusion; the conclusion is meant to follow from these reasons. The primary task of logic is to distinguish between good arguments (those in which the premises really do support, imply, provide evidence for, or make reasonable to believe the conclusion) and bad arguments (those in which the premises do not in fact support, etc. the conclusion, even though the argument purports that they do so).

In analyzing arguments, it is crucial to distinguish premises from conclusions. Sometimes premises precede the conclusion, but sometimes they do not. In order to distinguish premises from conclusions, one must understand the relation that the statements in an argument have to each other. This relation is often signaled by certain *indicator words*, such as "therefore," "hence," and "so," which indicate conclusions, and "because," "since," and "for," which indicate premises.

A first step in analyzing an argument is to restructure it, putting the premises first and the conclusion last. Thus, the argument "Socrates must be mortal, since he is a man and all men are mortal" may be restructured as:

> Socrates is a man.   *premises*
> All men are mortal.
>
> Therefore, Socrates is mortal.   *conclusion*

Notice that the clause "he is a man" in the original argument has been replaced by the sentence "Socrates is a man" in the restructured argument. This reflects the fact that in arguments *statements* are used to express *propositions*, the meaning-contents of statements. Thus, when the work "he" is used to refer to Socrates, the statements "he is a man" and "Socrates is a man" express the same proposition; that is, they have the same meaning-content. If we want to be subtle, we can say that arguments consist of propositions but they are expressed by statements. In practice, however, we can typically ignore the distinction between propositions and statements, provided that we are careful to understand and accurately reexpress the meanings of the statements in the argument.

Notice also that the word "must" in "Socrates must be mortal" is used as an indicator of the status of the statement "Socrates is mortal" as a conclusion. The premises are not meant to show that "Socrates *has to be* mortal," in the sense that it is impossible that he be otherwise; what *has to be* is that he *is* mortal *if* he is a man and all men are mortal. The word "since" in the original argument is used as an indicator of both of the premises.

1

Sample Exercises from Exercise 1.1. Part I

1. Titanium combines readily with oxygen, nitrogen, and hydrogen, all of which have an adverse effect on its mechanical properties. As a result, titanium must be processed in their absence.

   Restructured form:

   P₁: Titanium combines readily with oxygen, nitrogen, and hydrogen.
   P₂: Oxygen, nitrogen, and hydrogen have an adverse effect on the mechanical properties of titanium.
   C: Titanium must be processed in the absence of oxygen, nitrogen, and hydrogen.

   In this example, the words "as a result" indicate the conclusion. The student should realize that this example might be construed as an *explanation* of why titanium must be processed in the indicated way, rather than construed as an argument at all.

2. Since the good, according to Plato, is that which furthers a person's real interests, it follows that in any given case, when the good is known, men will seek it.

   Restructured form:

   P: The good is that which furthers a person's real interests.
   C: In any given case, when the good is known, men will seek it.

   In this example, the words "it follows that" indicate the conclusion of Plato's argument; the word "Since" indicates the premise. Notice that in restructuring the argument, it is the argument attributed *to* Plato that is expressed. As we shall see in the following section, this entire example is really a *report of* Plato's argument rather than *being* an argument itself.

3. As the denial or perversion of justice by the sentences of courts, as well as in any other manner, is with reason classed among the just causes of war, it will follow that the federal judiciary ought to have cognizance of all causes in which the citizens of other countries are concerned.

   Restructured form:

   P₁: The denial or perversion of justice by the sentences of courts, as well as in any other manner, is among the just causes of war.
   C: The federal judiciary ought to have cognizance of all causes in which the citizens of other countries are concerned.

4. When individuals voluntarily abandon property, they forfeit any expectation of privacy in it that they might have had. Therefore a warrantless search or seizure of abandoned property is not unreasonable under the Fourth Amendment.

   Restructured form:

   P: When individuals abandon property, they forfeit any expectation of privacy in it that they might have had.
   C: A warrantless search or seizure of abandoned property is not unreasonable under the Fourth Amendment.

   The indicator word "Therefore" makes this an easy example to restructure.

2

Put the following arguments into a restructured form, indicating premises and conclusion and placing premises first.

1. Only a fool or a daredevil smokes cigarettes, since cigarette smoking is a leading cause of cancer.

2. If we had world enough and time, this coyness would not be a crime. But we don't have world enough and time. So this coyness is a crime.

3. The square root of the number two is an irrational number. It follows that the hypotenuse of an isosceles right triangle is not commensurable with its side.

4. No man is an island. Every man is a piece of the continent, a part of the main. Therefore, no one should send to know for whom the bell tolls.

5. A free market is necessary for a free society. For without the freedom to buy and sell, the freedom to speak is absent. Moreover, in the absence of a free market, tyranny flourishes.

6. He jests at scars that never felt a wound. So Mercutio must never have felt a wound, since he jests at scars.

7. The French are the most intelligent people in the world. For it takes years and years for adult Americans to lean to speak the French language well. But in France even little children speak it well.

8. The world must have existed from eternity. For it not, then at some time there was nothing at all. And out of nothing at all nothing at all could come.

9. The world must have existed from eternity. Therefore, since eternity includes 6006 B.C., the world must have existed in 6006 B.C.

10. There are many average families in the United States. It follows that many U.S. families have parts of children in them, because the average U.S. family has 2.2 children and two-tenths of a child is a part of a child.

1.2 RECOGNIZING ARGUMENTS

It is important to distinguish arguments from nonargumentative passages. In an argument, at least one of the statements must present evidence, and there must be a claim, implicit or explicit, that something follows from the evidence. Words that are indicators of premises and conclusions are useful clues to, but not guarantees of, the presence of an argument. Typical indicator words can function to signal passages of sorts other than arguments, and arguments may contain no indicator words. "I don't like ice cream because the cold hurts my teeth" contains the indicator word "because," but it is an explanation, not an argument. "The banning of British beef is necessary; mad cow disease is highly contagious and extremely dangerous, and mad cow disease has appeared in British cattle" is an argument, even though it contains no indicator words.

Typical kinds of nonarguments are *warnings, pieces of advice, statements of belief or opinion, descriptions, loosely associated statements, reports, expository passages, illustrations, conditional statements,* and *explanations.*

Illustrations, conditional statements, and explanations are the types of nonarguments most apt to be confused with arguments. Illustrations can be confused with arguments because they often contain the word "thus," one of the typical indicator words. Here is an example: "Many painters have taken as their real subject some abstract theme. Thus, Goya and Picasso, each in his own way—Goya's *The Disasters of War* series and Picasso's painting *Guernica*—explores the pain and horror of warfare." The idea of this passage is to illustrate a general point, not to prove it.

A conditional statement is an "if . . . then" statement, such as "If the air pressure lowers, then the barometer falls." The statement immediately following the "if" (here "the air pressure lowers") is called the *antecedent* of the conditional; the statement following the "then" (here "the barometer falls") is called the *consequent.* Occasionally, the word "then" in a conditional statement may be omitted. Conditional statements look like arguments; that is, a conditional statement looks like an argument in which the antecedent is the premise and the consequent is the conclusion. But in a conditional statement no commitment is being made, even imaginatively, to the truth either of the antecedent or of the consequent. What the conditional asserts is merely that *if* the antecedent is true, the consequent is true. In an argument, however, some sort of commitment—even if only for the sake of arguing—is made to the truth of the premises.

One reason conditional statements look like arguments is that they express a transition in thought from one statement, the antecedent, to another, the consequent. An argument also expresses such a transition from its premises to its conclusion. In fact, the transition expressed in a conditional sentence may be reexpressed in the form of an argument that has the antecedent of the conditional as its premise and the consequent as its conclusion. For instance, the transition in the conditional "If the air pressure lowers, then the barometer falls" can be reexpressed in the form of an argument: "The air pressure lowers. Therefore, the barometer falls."

Even though conditional statements are not by themselves arguments, they may serve as premises or conclusions of arguments. Here is an argument containing a conditional statement as a premise:

> If the air pressure lowers, then the barometer falls.
> The air pressure just lowered.
> Therefore, the barometer just fell.

Here is an argument containing a conditional statement as conclusion:

> The higher the altitude, the lower the air pressure.
> At higher altitudes the barometer falls.
> We may conclude that if the air pressure lowers, then the barometer falls.

Explanations may be confused with arguments because they typically contain such indicator words as "because" or "for the reason that." Also explanations, like arguments, consist of two components: The *explanandum* (the state or event that is explained—or, more precisely, the description of this state or event) and the *explanans* (the statements that do the explaining). Thus, in "I don't like ice cream because the cold hurts my teeth," the *explanandum* is "I don't like ice cream" and the *explanans* is "the cold hurts my teeth." Explanations are not arguments because they do not claim to prove or justify that something is the case. In "I don't like ice cream because the cold hurts my teeth," it is not being claimed that my not liking ice cream is proven or demonstrated. My not liking ice cream is taken for granted; what the explanation does is to account for *why* I don't like ice cream. Arguments purport to *prove* something; explanations purport to *shed light on* something.

4

Sample Exercises from Exercise 1.2. Part I

1. The price of gold increased yesterday because of increased tensions in the Middle East.

   As typically spoken or written, this passage would not be an argument. It would be already known and taken for granted *that* the price of gold increased yesterday, so the point of the passage would not be to establish this fact. Rather, the passage attempts to explain *why* the price of gold increased.

2. If public education fails to improve the quality of instruction in both primary and secondary schools, then it is likely that it will lose additional students to the private sector in the years ahead.

   Here no commitment is made to the truth of the statement that public education will fail to improve the quality of instruction in both primary and secondary schools. The passage simply states that *if* this happens *then* it is likely that public education will lose additional students to the private sector in the years ahead. The passage is not an argument but rather a conditional statement.

3. Freedom of the press is the most important of our constitutionally guaranteed freedoms. Without it, our other freedoms would be immediately threatened. Furthermore, it provides the fulcrum for the advancement of new freedoms.

   This passage clearly claims to prove something, namely that freedom of the press is the most important of our constitutionally guaranteed freedoms. The first statement of the passage is thus the conclusion of the argument the passage constitutes, and the remaining two statements present the premises for this conclusion.

4. Water is a good solvent for many different substances, and it picks them up as it moves through the environment. Thus, rain water flowing over and under the ground dissolves minerals such as limestone.

   This passage does not attempt to prove that rain water flowing over and under the ground dissolves minerals such as limestone. Rather, the second sentence of the passage exemplifies the general statement made by its first sentence.

Additional Exercises for Section 1.2

Determine whether the following passages constitute arguments. For each argument, identify its conclusion.

1. The reason the beaker exploded is that it contained nitroglycerin and was shaken violently.

2. The reason it is undoubtable that there are flying saucers is that many people have seen them with their own eyes.

3. John did not feel very lively, so he probably ate something that did not agree with him.

4. John did not feel very lively, so he stayed home from the dance.

5. If you want a cup of coffee, you may have one.

6. If you want a cup of coffee, you are addicted to caffeine.

7. Several nations now possess the technology to manufacture nuclear weapons, even though they may not actually have built such weapons. Thus, South Africa, North Korea, Iraq, and Israel all have a number of atomic power plants and many laboratories in which fissionable material may be isolated.

8. Several nations now possess the technology to manufacture nuclear weapons, even though they may not actually have built such weapons. Thus, the world is in much greater danger of a nuclear confrontation than one might at first think.

9. Prices escalate almost daily. This inflationary tendency in our economy is one of its most disturbing features. No one wants to have to pay more for an item tomorrow than he or she pays for it today.

10. Prices escalate almost daily. This inflationary tendency in our economy is one of its most disturbing features. A government cannot be considered responsible if it does not deal with this problem.

1.3 DEDUCTION AND INDUCTION

Arguments may be divided into two classes: deductive and inductive. When an argument has the purport of proving its conclusion *necessarily* from the premises, then it is best considered as a *deductive* argument. When an argument has the purport of showing its conclusion to be *likely* or *probable* given the premises, then it is best considered as an *inductive* argument. We may express this idea also in the following way. An argument is deductive if its purport is that it is *impossible* that its premises be true and its conclusion false. An argument is inductive if its purport is merely that it is *improbable* that its premises be true and its conclusion false.

In deciding whether an argument is deductive or inductive, several factors must be borne in mind. First, there is the nature of the link between premises and conclusion. If the conclusion follows, or is thought to follow necessarily from the premises, the argument is best regarded as deductive. Otherwise it is usually better to regard the argument as inductive. Second, special indicator words should be taken into account. In drawing its conclusion, if the argument employs such words as "necessarily," "certainly," or "absolutely," it is usually best regarded as deductive. If words such as "probably," "likely," or "plausibly" are employed, the argument is usually best regarded as inductive. Third, the form of the argument helps determine whether it is deductive or inductive. For example, arguments based on mathematics, arguments from definition, and arguments framed as syllogisms (categorical syllogisms, hypothetical syllogisms, and disjunctive syllogisms, all of which will be studied later) are best treated as deductive. These are several common types of inductive arguments, including *predictions about the future, arguments from analogy, inductive generalizations,* (many) *arguments from authority, arguments based on signs,* and *causal inferences.*

In a *prediction about the future,* the premises refer to matters in the present or past, and the conclusion is about some matter in the future. An *argument from analogy* depends on the existence of a similarity between two things or states of affairs. For example, someone might conclude that ostriches can fly because they have wings, and other creatures with wings are known to fly. An *inductive generalization* argues from knowledge about a sample of a group of things to a claim about the entire group. An (inductive) *argument from authority* appeals to some presumed authority, expert, or witness. An *argument based on signs* proceeds from the knowledge of a certain sign to a knowledge of the thing or situation that sign signifies. For example, from a sign saying "Danger" one might conclude that the area in which the sign is located contains something dangerous. *Causal inferences* argue from knowledge of causes to claims about effects, or conversely from knowledge of effects to claims about causes. If I conclude, from knowledge that a tornado hit a certain town, that the damage in the town was extensive, I argue from cause to effect. If I argue from the presence of ashes on the carpet to the claim that someone was smoking in the room, I argue from effect to cause.

Sample Exercises from Exercise 1.3. Part I

1. Because triangle A is congruent with triangle B, and triangle A is isosceles, it follows that triangle B is isosceles.

   This argument, like most arguments in mathematics, is best interpreted as deductive. The point of the argument is to provide absolutely that triangle B is isosceles, for it states that triangle A is isosceles and that triangle B coincides with it in every respect—that is, that B may be placed in A's position and they would coincide point for point (that is the meaning of the word "congruent"). Even though the likeness between A and B is appealed to in this argument, it is still *not* an argument from analogy, for the gist of the argument makes it clear that the conclusion is meant to follow necessarily from the premises.

2. The plaque on the Leaning Tower of Pisa says that Galileo performed experiments there with falling objects. It must be the case that Galileo did indeed perform those experiments there.

   This argument proceeds from a sign to what the sign signifies and is thus an inductive argument based on signs. It is not reasonably considered as deductive because it is not reasonably thought that a sign *necessarily* has to tell the truth. It is not a causal inference because it is not reasonably thought that Galileo's performing his experiments is the cause of the plaque's being in place.

3. The rainfall in Seattle has been over 15 inches every year for the past 30 years. There-fore, the rainfall next year will probably be over 15 inches.

   This argument is inductive, as the word "probably" indicates. It is a prediction about the future.

4. All street gangs are organizations involved in crime, and some street gangs are not clans shrouded in romance. Therefore, some organizations involved in crime are not clans shrouded in romance.

   This argument is best considered as a deductive argument because of its format. It has the form of a categorical syllogism (see text).

Additional Exercises for Section 1.3

Determine whether the following arguments are deductive or inductive; if an argument is inductive, identify its type.

1. Texans must all wear cowboy boots; I went to Houston last Thursday and everyone I saw on the street had boots on.

2. Even numbers yield even numbers when they are squared. It follows that the square roots of odd perfect squares are odd.

3. We can go out of the theater at the front; the Exit sign points in that direction.

4. Look at these footprints in the mud by the window. We must have a peeping tom.

5. This fish looks very similar to a trout or a salmon. Since those fish are tasty, this one must be tasty, too.

6. Of course the sun will rise tomorrow—it's risen every day in human history.

7. Everyone who is well educated knows about the existence of the Roman Empire, and John is well educated. So he has to know something about the Roman Empire.

8. Everyone who has ever tried to climb the Matterhorn has experienced terror at some stage of the ascent. Just you wait, John; sooner or later on your climb you are going to be afraid.

9. If you found a model of the solar system, you'd know that someone made it. How much more obvious it is, then, that the real solar system must have been made by somebody.

10. This circle has an area of exactly 4 square inches. So a circle with an area of 1 square inch would have a radius half as long.

1.4 VALIDITY, TRUTH, SOUNDNESS, STRENGTH, COGENCY

A deductive argument is either *valid* or *invalid*. Validity does not admit of amount or degree: an argument is either valid, period, or invalid, period; there is no middle ground. A deductive argument is valid if the conclusion follows necessarily from the premises—that is, if it is necessarily the case that if the premises were to be true (whether they are in fact true or not), the conclusion would have to be true (whether it is in fact true or not). Otherwise, a deductive argument is invalid. If there is any possibility that the premises could all be true and yet the conclusion false, then the argument is invalid.

Notice that true premises and a true conclusion are not required for validity. Indeed, there can be valid arguments with false premises and a false conclusion—for example, "Dogs have five legs; therefore, dogs have an odd number of legs." The only possibility ruled out by the validity of an argument is that it have all true premises and a false conclusion. Also notice that true premises and a true conclusion do not by any means ensure validity. There are invalid arguments with true premises and a true conclusion—for example, "Dogs have four legs; therefore, birds have two legs."

A *sound argument* is a deductive argument that is valid and has all true premises. Obviously, in a sound argument the conclusion will be true, too.

An inductive argument is either *strong* or *weak*. Unlike validity, the strength of an inductive argument *does* admit of amount or degree; an inductive argument A and an inductive argument B may both be strong and yet A may be stronger than B. For example, suppose A is "Ninety percent of the mice in Australia have been examined and found to be white; therefore probably all of the mice in Australia are white." This is a strong argument. But if B is "Ninety-nine percent of the mice in Australia have been examined and found to be white; therefore, probably all of the mice in Australia are white," then B is even stronger than A. An inductive argument is strong if on the basis of the assumption that its premises are true, its conclusion probably is true; otherwise, it is weak. An inductive argument having true premises but a probably false conclusion is weak; but aside from this fact strength and weakness have no more direct relation to the truth or falsity of premises and conclusion than do the validity and invalidity of deductive arguments.

A *cogent* argument is an inductive argument that is strong and has all true premises. Obviously, in a cogent argument the conclusion will probably be true, too.

Sample Exercises from Exercise 1.4. Part I

1. Since *Moby Dick* was written by Shakespeare, and *Moby Dick* is a science fiction novel, it follows that Shakespeare wrote a science fiction novel.

   Both premises of this argument are false; therefore, the argument is clearly not sound. However, the argument is nevertheless valid, because if it were the case that Shakespeare wrote *Moby Dick* and that *Moby Dick* were a science fiction novel, then it would have to be the case that Shakespeare wrote a science fiction novel.

2. If George Washington was beheaded, then George Washington died. George Washington died. Therefore, George Washington was beheaded.

   We may safely regard both premises of this argument to be true. The conclusion, however, is false. No valid argument can have true premises and a false conclusion, so this argument is invalid. all invalid arguments are unsound, so this one is unsound.

Sample exercises from Exercise 1.4. Part II

1. This die is marked with numbers 1 through 6. Therefore, probably the next roll will turn up a 6.

   In this inductive argument the premise is true (as we know from the instructions to the exercise.) The conclusion, however, is probably false, because there is only one way the die can turn up a 6 and there are five ways it can fail to turn up a 6. Therefore, this is a weak inductive argument, and as such it is not cogent.

2. This die is marked with numbers 1 through 6. Therefore, probably the next roll will turn up a number less than 6.

   The premise is true in this argument. The conclusion is probably true because there are five ways the die can turn up a number less than 6 and there is only one way it can fail to turn up a number less than 6. So this is a strong inductive argument. Since it also has a true premise (its only premise), it is a cogent argument.

Additional Exercises for Section 1.4

Determine whether the following arguments are deductive or inductive. If the argument is deductive, determine whether it is valid or invalid. If the argument is inductive, determine whether it is strong or weak.

1. This is a standard deck of playing cards. So probably if I draw a card at random from it, that card will be a king.

2. This is a standard deck of playing cards. So if I draw a card at random from it, fifty-one cards will remain.

3. This is a standard deck of playing cards. So if I draw a card at random from it, that card will probably not be a spade.

4. We know that the murderer was either Jackson or Harrison. We also know the murderer could not have been Harrison. so the murderer had to be Jackson.

5. We know that the murderer was either Jackson or Harrison. So probably the murderer was Jackson.

6. Every number evenly divisible by 4 is evenly divisible by 2. Therefore, no number evenly divisible by 4 is odd.

7. If dogs have more than five legs, then they have more than four legs. Dogs do not have more than five legs. Therefore, dogs do not have more than four legs.

8. John has a favorite color among those in the spectrum. So it is probably red.

9. For quite a while every fourth United States president has died while in office. Ronald Reagan is the fourth president after Kennedy, who died in office. It is likely, then, that Ronald Reagan will die in office.

10. Every sample of copper ever examined conducts electricity. So it is a safe bet that this particular piece of copper will conduct electricity when we examine it.

1.5   ARGUMENT FORMS: PROVING INVALIDITY

The validity of an argument is to a large extent independent of its subject matter and is, instead, dependent on the *form* or *structure* of the argument. For instance, consider the argument form

> All *A* are *B*.
> All *B* are *C*.
> Therefore, all *A* are *C*.

where *A*, *B*, and *C* stand for terms designating types of things. No matter what these letters stand for, the resulting argument will be a valid one. Thus, this is a *valid argument form*. An *invalid argument form* is one that has at least one substitution instance that is an invalid argument. (A *substitution instance* of an argument form in general is obtained by replacing the letters in an argument form by terms designating types of things or by statements.) Every substitution instance of a valid argument form is valid, while at least one substitution instance of an invalid argument form must be invalid; indeed, an invalid argument form must have at least one substitution instance in which its premises are actually true and its conclusion false.

We might adopt the following alternative definition of invalidity:

An argument is invalid if and only if its form allows for at least one substitution instance having true premises and a false conclusion.

This definition comprises two claims: (1) An argument is invalid if and only if it has an invalid form and is not a substitution instance of any valid form; (2) an argument form is invalid if and only if it has at least one substitution instance in which the premises are true and the conclusion false.

It follows from this alternate definition of invalidity that an argument may be proved invalid by first isolating its logical form and then inventing a substitution instance of this form with true premises and a false conclusion. This method is called the *counterexample* method. For example, the argument

> All elms are plants.
> All trees are plants.
> Therefore, all elms are trees.

has the form

> All A are B.
> All C are B.
> Therefore, all A are C.

But this form has the substitution instance:

> All horses are animals.
> All cows are animals.
> Therefore, all horses are cows.

This argument has true premises and a false conclusion, which shows that the original argument was invalid.

Note of caution: Consider the following valid argument:

> This object is red.
> Therefore, this object is not green.

This argument has the form:

> This object is A.
> Therefore, this object is not B.

But this form has the following substitution instance:

> This object is a stallion.
> Therefore, this object is not a horse.

This is clearly an argument that has, in the right circumstances, a true premise and a false conclusion. The procedure used here would show, incorrectly, that the original argument was not valid. The point here is that using the counterexample method may be complicated and that it may depend on the meanings of the terms involved in the argument. As one more example of how difficult it may be to use the counterexample method, consider the following two

11

arguments, noting the fact that the first one is valid and that the second one has true premises and a false conclusion:

> If Madonna is the wife of Boris Yeltsin, then she is married to him.
> Madonna is not the wife of Boris Yeltsin.
> Therefore, she is not married to him.

> If Madonna is the daughter of Boris Yeltsin, then she is younger than he.
> Madonna is not the daughter of Boris Yeltsin
> Therefore, she is not younger than he.

Sample Exercises from Section 1.5. Part I

1. All galaxies are structures that contain black holes in the center, so all galaxies are quasars, since all quasars are structures that contain black holes in the center.

    This argument has the form

    > All *G* are *S*.
    > All *Q* are *S*.
    > Therefore, all *G* are *Q*.

    Substitution instance:

    > All dogs are mammals.
    > All cats are mammals.
    > Therefore, all dogs are cats.

2. Some evolutionists are not persons who believe in the Bible, for no creationists are evolutionists, and some persons who believe in the Bible are not creationists.

    This argument has the form

    > No *C* are *E*.
    > Some *P* are not *C*.
    > Therefore, some *E* are not *P*.

    Substitution instance:

    > No fish are mammals.
    > Some animals are not fish.
    > Therefore, some mammals are not animals.

3. No patents are measures that discourage research and development, and all patents are regulations that protect intellectual property. Thus no measures that discourage research and development are regulations that protect intellectual property.

    This argument has the form

    > No *P* are *M*.
    > All *P* are *R*.
    > Therefore, no *M* are *R*.

Substitution instance:

> No dogs are cats.
> All dogs are animals.
> Therefore, no cats are animals.

4. Some farm workers are not persons who are paid decent wages, because no illegal aliens are persons who are paid decent wages, and some illegal aliens are not farm workers.

This argument has the form:

> No *I* are *P*.
> Some *I* are not *F*.
> Therefore, some *F* are not *P*.

Substitution instance:

> No fish are mammals.
> Some fish are not cats.
> Therefore, some cats are not mammals.

Additional Exercises for Section 1.5

Identify the form of each of the following arguments and use it to determine whether each argument is valid or invalid. If an argument is invalid, construct a substitution instance of its form in which all the premises are true and the conclusion is false.

1. All fish are vertebrates and all vertebrates belong to the animal kingdom, so all fish belong to the animal kingdom.

2. All fish are vertebrates and some bass are fish. Therefore, some bass are vertebrates.

3. All fish are vertebrates and some bass are vertebrates. Therefore, some bass are fish.

4. No grasshoppers are butterflies, but all monarchs are butterflies. So no grasshoppers are monarchs.

5. No grasshoppers are butterflies, but some moths are butterflies. So no moths are grasshoppers.

6. Some logicians are philosophers, and some logicians are mathematicians. It follows that some philosophers are mathematicians.

7. Some existentialist poets are geniuses, for some madmen are existentialist poets and all geniuses are madmen.

8. Some lovers of music are trombone players. It follows that some trombone players are not jazz musicians, since no jazz musicians are lovers of music.

9. All the brave deserve the fair. None that deserve the fair are faint-hearted. We may conclude that none of the brave are faint-hearted.

10. All tasks are challenges to the industrious. All tasks are burdens to the lazy. Therefore, all challenges to the industrious are burdens to the lazy.

1.6 EXTENDED ARGUMENTS

Extended arguments, such as those found in editorials, essays, religious and political tracts, and the like, are often difficult to analyze. Not only are premises and conclusions sometimes difficult to identify, but the skeleton of the argument is frequently obscured by rhetorical embellishments, illustrations, explanations, statements of opinion, and emotional appeals, as well as a host of other sorts of expository prose. Extended arguments may consist of a string of subarguments, with conclusions of some subarguments functioning as premises of other subarguments. Premises and conclusions are often suppressed in extended arguments and left for the reader to provide or presuppose. Although there is no simple technique for examining extended argumentation, several devices can be used in an extended argument analysis.

First, it is helpful to number the separate statements in an extended argument; the numbers can then be referenced in order to discuss the statements without undue prolixity. Second, arrows can be inserted to indicate the relation of evidential or inferential support, as follows:

This diagram says that statement ② supports statement ①. Third, braces indicate conjoint support either by premises or of conclusions. Thus the diagram

illustrates that ② and ③ conjointly support ①. The diagram

says, on the other hand, that each of ② and ③ supports ① independently. The diagram

says that ① supports both ② and ③. It is in fact equivalent to the following pair of diagrams.

A fourth device useful to illustrate the structure of some extended arguments is the equals sign. Thus, the diagram

$$① = ②$$

says that numerals 1 and 2 are attached to essentially the same statement (in technical language: the same proposition).

1. ① The conditions under which many food animals are raised are unhealthy for humans. ② To keep these animals alive, large quantities of drugs must be administered. ③ These drugs remain in the animals' flesh and are passed on to the humans who eat it.

   In this argument, premise ② and premise ③ function conjointly to support the conclusion ①. The diagram for the argument is thus as follows:

2. ① The development of carbon-embedded plastics, otherwise called "composits," is an important new technology because ② it holds the key for new aircraft and spacecraft designs. ③ This is so because these composits are not only stronger than steel but lighter than aluminum.

   In this argument ③ supports ②, while ② in turn supports ①. Hence, the argument is to be diagrammed as:

3. ① Homework stifles the thrill of learning in the mind of the student. ② It instills an oppressive learn-or-else discipline. ③ It quenches the desire for knowledge and the love of truth. ④ For these reasons homework should never be assigned.

   In this argument the conclusion, as is clearly indicated by the words "For these reasons," is ④. The student may have some doubt about whether the premises ①, ②, and ③ support the conclusion ④ conjointly or independently; but the words "For *these* reasons" suggest that *conjoint* support is intended. The diagram for this argument should, accordingly, be

4. ① When parents become old and destitute, the obligation of caring for them should be imposed on their children. ② Clearly, children owe a debt to their parents. ③ Their parents brought them into the world and cared for them when they were unable to care for themselves. ④ This debt could be appropriately discharged by having grown children care for their parents.

   In this argument ① is the conclusion of the argument; it is what the whole argument purports to show. In support of this conclusion, the argument offers the conjoint support of premises ② and ④. In turn, ② is itself supported by ③. Thus the diagram of this argument looks like this:

Additional Exercises for Section 1.6

Using the devices introduced in this Section, construct diagrams of the following arguments.

1. ① The man who broke into this warehouse must have been rather heavy. ② His footprints sink at least an inch into this dry soil, and ③ his shoe size is at least a thirteen. Moreover, ④ we can see by where he bumped his head on this rafter that he is at least six and a half feet tall.

2. ① The population of the world increases, as Malthus said, far out of proportion to the world's food supply. ② Indeed, it can be maintained that the world's food supply is approaching a theoretical maximum, for ③ the world's arable land is at present nearly all cultivated, and ④ technology promises very little in the way of increasing the land's productivity. It is obvious, therefore, that ⑤ population control is one of the world's most pressing problems.

3. ① Modern war must be total war, for ② modern weaponry demands that battle must be pushed to the technological extreme if it is to be won and ③ no one wages war without the intention to win. But since ④ total war implies total destruction and ⑤ total destruction is incompatible with civilized life, ⑥ pacifism is the only consistent moral and social policy.

4. ① The legacy of the past is the directive of the present. ② Our social ills, as everyone recognizes, are passed from one generation to the next. ③ The means of the present are, however, the hard-won lessons of the past: ④ we ignore history only to repeat it. ⑤ It is clear, then, that a study of history is a prerequisite for a rational life in the present.

5. ① The development of the human fetus from conception to birth is a qualitatively continuous process. ② There are no sudden leaps in either mental or physical fetal maturation. ③ Clearly the end of fetal development is a human being, and ④ the treatment of human beings is clearly the paramount concern of the moral enterprise. Because ⑤ the treatment of human beings is so crucial morally, and because ⑥ no lines can be drawn between what is and is not a human being, ⑦ moral circumspection requires that we treat the fetus in any stage of development as if it were a human being.

2
LANGUAGE: MEANING
AND DEFINITION

2.1 COGNITIVE MEANING AND EMOTIVE MEANING

Ordinary discourse employs language in many ways, but two prominent functions of language are to convey information and to evoke and express emotion. Although few words are used purely to express emotion ("ouch," "damn," when used as an expletive, for example), many words can have both an emotive and cognitive significance. The words "police officer" are perhaps emotively bare or neutral, but "peace officer," while conveying the very same cognitive notion, has a positive or honorific emotive overtone. "Cop," "bull," and "pig" are often used with the same cognitive import but each conveys a negative or pejorative emotive overtone.

The fact that many words have emotive meaning as well as cognitive meaning is important for the analysis of argument because an argument may be persuasive, not because of its intrinsic strength, but rather because its emotively-charged language is appealing. In politics, religion, advertising, and morals, emotively-invested language is heavily employed; in these areas of discourse especially, one must be on guard to avoid being taken in unawares by intrinsically weak argumentation.

Additional Exercises for Section 2.1

Each of the following words is emotively charged. Identify, for each, whether the emotive tone is predominantly positive or negative, and replace each with a more emotively neutral word.

1. valiant steed
2. broken-down nag
3. shyster
4. quack
5. hag
6. drunkard
7. senior citizen
8. jock
9. man of God
10. trusty firearm

2.2   THE INTENSION AND EXTENSION OF TERMS

A word is a *term* if it may be used as the subject of a statement. Terms consist of proper names, common names, and descriptive phrases. For example, "George Washington," "dog," and "house on the hill" are terms.

Terms have an *intensional meaning* and an *extensional meaning*. The intensional meaning, or *intension,* of a term is the qualities or attributes that the term *connotes* (and for this reason it is also called the *connotation* of the term). Note that in logic "connotation" has a different meaning than it does in linguistics, where "connotation" refers to the subtle nuances of a word. The extensional meaning, or *extension,* of a term is the members of the class of things that the term *denotes* (and for this reason is also called the *denotation* of the term).

A term has *empty extension* if there are no members of the class of things it denotes; for example, the term "werewolf" has empty extension. This is related to the fact that *intension determines extension:* a thing is a member of the class a term denotes if and only if it has the qualities that the term connotes. It follows that there are no meaningful terms with empty intensions—if a term does not connote any qualities at all, it is meaningless, and thus it would be impossible to determine its extension.

Terms may be put in an order: an order of increasing intension, increasing extension, decreasing intension, or decreasing extension. A series of terms is in order of increasing intension when each term in the series (except the first) connotes more qualities than the previous term. A series of terms is in order of increasing extension when each term in the series (except the first) denotes a class that includes both all the members of the class denoted by the previous term and also other things not in that class. The terms "number," "even number," and "even number greater than 2" are in order of increasing intension, while the terms "even number greater than 2," "even number," and "number" are in order of increasing extension. This example illustrates that increasing intension often corresponds with decreasing extension, and vice-versa. But this correspondence is not absolutely necessary or always the case. (See the text for examples in which this correspondence does not obtain.)

Sample Exercises from Exercise 2.2. Part I

1. "Extortion," "practitioner," "seriousness," "scarlet," "reinvestment," "Thomas Jefferson," "Empire State Building," "graceful dancer," "tallest man on the squad," and "mountaintop" are clearly capable of being used as the subject of a statement; so they are clearly terms. "Laborious," "cunningly," "interestingly impassive," "therefore," "annoy," "render satisfactory," "wake up," "not only," "between," and "since" clearly cannot serve as the subject of a statement and so are not terms. "Forever" is defined by the dictionary as an adverb, and in this sense it cannot be a term. However, "forever" is sometimes used in the sense of "eternity" ("Forever is a long, long time"), and in this sense it is a term. Because the phrase "whoever studies" can be used as the subject of a sentence (e.g., "Whoever studies will learn"), it fits the criterion for being a term.

4. The following are in order of increasing intension:
   a. Plant, tree, conifer, spruce, Sitka spruce.
   b. Vehicle, car, sports car, Italian sports car, Maserati.
   c. Person, professional person, Doctor of Medicine, surgeon, brain surgeon.
   d. Animal, mammal, marsupial, kangaroo, wallaby.
   e. Polygon, quadrilateral, parallelogram, rectangle, square.

Additional Exercises for Section 2.2

1. Construct a series of four terms of increasing intension.

2. Construct a series of four terms of increasing extension.

3. Construct a series of terms of decreasing intension.

4. Construct a series of terms of decreasing extension.

5. Describe the following series as to intension and extension: implement, farm implement, hoe.

6. Try to give the intension of the following terms: triangle, right triangle, isosceles triangle, equilateral triangle.

7. Identify the extension of each of the following terms: ghost, number that equals its own square, last king of France, rational number whose square is 2, perfect square number between 1 and 100.

8. What elements are common to the intensions of the following pairs of terms?
   a. square, triangle
   b. square, equilateral triangle
   c. horse, cow
   d. chair, book

9. Give five terms with empty extension.

10. Give five terms whose extension consists of exactly one item.

2.3   DEFINITIONS AND THEIR PURPOSES

Definitions are intended to explicate the meanings of words. Every definition consists of a *definiendum* (the word or group of words that is supposed to be defined by the definition) and a *definiens* (the word or group of words that does the defining). The definiens symbolizes the same meaning as the definiendum. Definitions may be of various types. A *stipulative definition* assigns a meaning to a word for the first time. (The word may already have other standard meanings, but the stipulative definition assigns a new meaning to the word.) This assignment, though there may be some rationale for it, is essentially arbitrary: it is independent of any prior meanings the word may have had. Consequently, there is no such thing as a true or false stipulative definition. A *lexical definition* is used to report the meaning or meanings that a word already has. Dictionaries consist of lexical definitions. Accordingly, a lexical definition, unlike a stipulative definition, can be true or false: it is true if it correctly reports the meaning the word already has; otherwise, it is false.

Another sort of definition is a *precising definition,* which has the purpose of reducing the vagueness of a word. (Vagueness must be distinguished from ambiguity: a word is *vague* if it is not clear just what the word means in every case; a word is *ambiguous* if it has two or more distinct, clear meanings. For example, "democracy" is vague, while "saw"—which can mean both the past tense of "see" and the wood-cutting tool—is ambiguous or at least is susceptible to ambiguous usage.) Precising definitions are often found, for example, in legal texts. Like stipulative definitions, precising definitions involve a new assignment of meaning; but, unlike stipulative definitions, precising definitions do not assign meaning arbitrarily.

A *theoretical definition* provides a theoretical characterization of the thing denoted by its *definiendum.* It provides a way of conceiving that thing that has deductive consequences in the theory at hand. The definition of "work" as "force multiplied by the distance over which the force is exerted" is a theoretical definition used in physics. Not all theoretical definitions occur in science; some, for example, occur in philosophy, art criticism, and other theoretical disciplines. Like stipulative definitions, theoretical definitions are neither true nor false, at least not in any simple sense of these terms.

A *persuasive definition* has the purpose of creating a favorable or unfavorable attitude toward the thing denoted by its definiendum. Persuasive definitions are offered as if they were merely lexical definitions, but they contain value-laden elements that are intended to have a persuasive effect. "Democracy is the governing of responsible people by themselves" is a persuasive definition that is designed to engender a positive attitude; "democracy is the rule of the mob" is a persuasive definition that is designed to engender a negative attitude.

Sample Exercises from Exercise 2.3. Part I

1. "Blind" means, for federal income tax purposes, either the inability to see better than 20/200 in the better eye with glasses or having a field of vision of 20 degrees or less.

   This is a stipulative definition of "blind."

2. "Football" means a sport in which modern-day gladiators brutalize one another while trying to move a ridiculously shaped "ball" from one end of the playing field to the other.

   This is a persuasive definition of "football."

Additional Exercises for Section 2.3

1. Invent opposing pairs of persuasive definitions for "religion."

2. How would you characterize the definition of "entropy" found in thermodynamics?

3. A mathematician defines a "group" as "a set of objects together with a binary relation, such that the set contains an identity element, the set is closed under the binary relation, every element of the set has an inverse in the set, and the binary relation is associative." What sort of definition is this?

4. "Death is the moment of the soul's liberation, the healing of the disease of life." What sort of definition is this?

5. "A lime is a small greenish citrus fruit, shaped like a lemon but usually smaller than a lemon." What sort of definition is this?

2.4   DEFINITIONAL TECHNIQUES

Techniques used to produce definitions may be classified into extensional techniques and intensional techniques. An *extensional definition* is one that assigns a meaning to a word by indicating the class of things that the definiendum denotes. An *intensional definition* is one that assigns a meaning to a word by indicating the qualities or attributes that the *definiendum* connotes.

Extensional definitions are of at least three types. A *demonstrative, or ostensive, definition* indicates the members of the definiendum's denotation by *pointing* to them. An *enumerative definition* indicates the members of the *definiendum's* denotation by *naming* them. A *definition by subclass* indicates the members of the *definiendum's* denotation by *naming subclasses* of this denotation. Extensional definitions are chiefly used as lexical or stipulative definitions. The main fault of extensional definitions is that they cannot guarantee that the intensional meaning of the *definiendum* is communicated.

Intensional definitions are of at least four types. In a *synonymous definition,* the *definiens* is a single word that connotes the very same attributes as the *definiendum.* An example is "A physician is a doctor." An *etymological definition* assigns a meaning to a word by giving that word's linguistic background or "ancestry." Languages are evolving phenomena, and words in any language have developed from linguistic forebears, either in that language or in other languages. Providing an account of such forebears of a word is often a useful way of specifying the most basic connotative ideas that make up the intension of a term. An *operational definition* assigns a meaning to a word by specifying experimental procedures that can be used to determine whether or not the *definiendum* applies to any given thing. An example is "A substance is a conductor if and only if, when a battery is connected to the ends of it, a nearby galvanometer deflects." A *definition by genus and difference* assigns a meaning to a term by specifying a genus word and one or more specific-difference words, which together provide the attributes that the *definiendum* connotes. In logic "genus" simply means a class, and "species" means a smaller subclass of a genus. A specific difference of a species is an attribute that distinguishes that species from other species in the genus. Thus, a species is indicated by giving its genus and its specific difference. If we define "foal" as a newborn horse, then we are employing a definition by genus and difference: the genus is "horse," and the specific difference is "newborn."

Sample Exercises from Exercise 2.4. Part I

1. "Plant" means something such as a tree, a flower, a vine, or a cactus. This is an enumerative definition.

2. "Hammer" means a tool used for pounding. This is a definition by genus (tool) and difference (used for pounding).

Additional Exercises for Section 2.4

1. Construct a definition by genus and difference of "square," "circle," "even number," and "odd number."

2. How would you characterize the following definition: "An object A is heavier than an object B if and only if, whenever A and B are placed in two dishes of a balance scale, A sinks and B rises."

3. What sort of definition is "An insect is an ant, a grasshopper, a butterfly, and so on"?

4. What sort of definition is "The color red is *that* color" (said while pointing to a certain color)?

5. Provide operational definitions for "ductile" and "malleable."

6. Give definitions by subclass for "marsupial" and "ungulate."

21

7. Can theoretical and stipulative definitions always be sharply distinguished?

8. Provide a definition for "junior college." What type is it?

9. Construct an enumerative definition of "planet."

10. What sort of definition is "A tenant is a dweller"?

2.5   CRITERIA FOR LEXICAL DEFINITIONS

The purpose of a lexical definition is to report the meaning a word has as it is actually used in a language. Lexical definitions may achieve this purpose to a greater or lesser degree. The following rules help evaluate lexical definitions.

Rule 1: A lexical definition should conform to the standards of proper grammar.

Rule 2: A lexical definition should convey the *essential* meaning of the word being defined. The attributes mentioned in the definition should be the important or necessary features of the thing defined, not trivial ones.

Rule 3: A lexical definition should be neither *too broad* nor *too narrow*. A definition is too broad if the definiens applies to things other than the things that are being defined. For instance, "A fish is a creature that swims in the ocean" is too broad because it includes whales and dolphins, which are not fish. A definition is too narrow if it does not apply to all the things that are being defined. For instance, the above definition of "fish" is too narrow because it does not apply to freshwater fish. Thus, a definition can be both too broad and too narrow.

Rule 4: A lexical definition should *avoid circularity*. A circular definition uses the *definiendum* in some way in the *definiens* and is thus not genuinely informative.

Rule 5: A lexical definition should not be *negative* when it can be affirmative. Nevertheless, some words, like "pristine" and "virginity," are intrinsically negative; for them, a negative definition is quite appropriate.

Rule 6: A lexical definition should *avoid figurative, obscure, vague,* or *ambiguous* language.

Rule 7: A lexical definition should *avoid affective terminology.*

Rule 8: A lexical definition should indicate the *context* to which the *definiens* pertains. For example, "mate" has one meaning in the context of a game of chess and quite another in the context of sailing.

Sample Exercises from Exercise 2.5

1. A sculpture is a three-dimensional image made of marble.

   This definition is too narrow in that it does not include sculptures made of iron, brass, or other materials.

2. "Elusory" means elusive.

   This definition is circular.

3. "Develop" means to transform by the action of chemicals.

   This definition fails to indicate the context (photography) to which the *definiens* pertains.

4. A cynic is a person who knows the price of everything and the value of nothing.—*Oscar Wilde*

   This definition makes use of sarcastic language. In addition, its use of the word "value" is vague.

Additional Exercises for Section 2.5

Use the eight rules for evaluating lexical definitions to criticize the following definitions.

1. A pony is a horse.

2. A horse is a large four-legged animal that is ridden and used to do work.

3. A flush is five cards of the same suit.

4. A table is a piece of furniture with four legs and a flat top.

5. A poem is a soul's prayer to reality.

6. A communist is a power-monger with a golden tongue.

7. The soul is the harmony of the body.

8. Knowledge is true belief.

9. Truth is a correspondence between an idea and the way things are.

10. A ball is a spheroid of nonutilitarian functionality.

3
INFORMAL FALLACIES

3.1 FALLACIES IN GENERAL

A *fallacy* is a defect in an argument other than its having false premises. Fallacies are usually divided into two types: formal and informal. A *formal fallacy* is a fallacy that may be identified by a mere inspection of the form of the argument. An argument having an invalid form, such as "All *A* are *B;* all *A* are *C;* therefore, all *B* are *C*," contains a formal fallacy. An *informal fallacy* is a fallacy that, in order to be identified, requires an analysis of the content of the argument and not just an inspection of its form. For example, "Bob Dole is no friend of mine; no friend of mine is a Chinese communist; therefore, Bob Dole is a Chinese communist" may appear to have a valid form, but it is clearly fallacious. Because detecting the fallaciousness of this argument depends on understanding its content—in particular the meaning of "no friend of mine"—the argument contains an informal fallacy.

Informal fallacies may be classified in a number of ways, and it would be presumptuous to claim that any particular classification is complete. The classification in the text contains twenty-two informal fallacies, divided into five groups: fallacies of relevance, fallacies of weak induction, fallacies of presumption, fallacies of ambiguity, and fallacies of grammatical analogy.

Sample Exercises from Exercise 3.1

1. If Rasputin was really mad, then he deceived Czar Nicholas II. Rasputin was not really mad. Therefore, he did not deceive Czar Nicholas II.

   This argument commits a formal fallacy because it instantiates the invalid form "If R, then D: not-R; therefore, not-D." This invalid argument form is known as the fallacy of denying the antecedent.

2. Everything that runs has feet. The Columbia River runs very swiftly. Therefore, the Columbia River has feet.

   This argument commits an informal fallacy because in order for its fallacious character to be identified we must analyze its content and not just make an inspection of its form. In particular, the first premise requires that the word "runs" in it means "runs with feet." But "runs" in the second premise cannot mean "runs with feet." This type of fallacy, as will be discussed later in this chapter, is known as an "equivocation."

Additional Exercises for Section 3.1

Try to identify the reason or reasons why each of the following arguments is fallacious.

1. Abortion is miscarriage. Abortion is also a matter of justice. Therefore, abortion is a miscarriage of justice.

2. Sloppy Joe's has the most eaten hamburgers in town. So don't go to Sloppy Joe's for a hamburger: you are likely to find a bite out of it.

3. You will find that if you kill a toad by the light of the full moon, any wart you have will sooner or later go away. So killing a toad by the light of the full moon is a cure for warts.

4. Fagin is a superb thief. Any thief is a man. It follows that Fagin is a superb man.

5. John is heavy-hearted today, so even if you are strong you probably will not be able to lift him.

3.2 FALLACIES OF RELEVANCE

The *fallacies of relevance* apply to arguments with premises that are not logically relevant to the conclusion but that are *psychologically* relevant to the conclusion in such a way as to make the conclusion *seem* to follow from them. In this section eight fallacies of relevance are presented.

1. The *appeal to force* (*argumentum and baculum*) occurs when the arguer, instead of providing genuine evidence for a conclusion, provides some sort of threat of harm to the listener or reader if the conclusion is not accepted.

2. The *appeal to pity* (*argumentum ad misericordiam*) occurs when the arguer, instead of providing genuine evidence for a conclusion, attempts to get the conclusion accepted by evoking pity from the listener or reader.

3. The *appeal to the people* (*argumentum ad populum*) occurs when the arguer, instead of providing genuine evidence for a conclusion, tries to get the conclusion accepted by playing upon the listener's or reader's desire to be loved, esteemed, admired, valued, recognized, or accepted by others. In the *direct approach,* the arguer tries to get a conclusion accepted by whipping up the collective enthusiasm of a crowd. In the *indirect approach,* the arguer directs the appeal to one or more individuals, concentrating on some aspect of their relation to a crowd or populace. The indirect approach includes the *bandwagon argument* (urging that someone "Jump on the bandwagon" so as not to be "left out" or "different"), the *appeal to vanity,* and the *appeal to snobbery.*

4. The *argument against the person* (*argumentum ad hominem*) occurs when one arguer directs his or her attention to the person of a second arguer and not to the second arguer's argument or position. The argument against the person occurs in three forms. In the *ad hominem abusive,* an arguer responds to another person's argument by verbally abusing of attacking that other person. In the *ad hominem circumstantial,* an arguer attempts to discredit his or her opponent's argument or position by calling attention to certain circumstances that affect the opponent, such as ways the opponent's self-interest is served by arguing as he or she does. In the *tu quoque* ("you too") type of ad hominem, the arguer attempts to defend himself or herself by alleging that the opponent is just as guilty. The *tu quoque* is sometimes called the "two wrongs make a right" fallacy.

5. The fallacy of *accident* is committed when a general rule is wrongly or unjustifiably applied to a specific case. For example, "Dogs have four legs; Fido just had one of his legs amputated; so Fido is not a dog any more," is a case of accident. The fallacy of accident often occurs in the context of morality, when general moral principles are hastily applied to specific cases. Here is an example: "Thou shalt not kill; therefore, it is morally wrong to use insecticides."

6. The fallacy of *straw man* occurs when an arguer distorts a certain argument or position for the purpose of more easily attacking it, refutes the distorted argument or position

(which is known as the "straw man" that the arguer has "set up"), and then concludes that the real argument or position has been refuted. The following argument against freedom of speech commits the straw man fallacy.

> Freedom of speech is not nearly as desirable as some people think. Why should anyone be allowed, for example, to incite others to violence, to make threatening phone calls, or to shout obscenities at policemen? And surely no one thinks people should be allowed to make fraudulent proposals, or to reveal military secrets to our enemies.

The real issue in freedom of speech is, of course, quite different from what this argument suggests.

7. The *fallacy of missing the point* (*ignoratio elenchi*) occurs when the premises of an argument lead, or seem to lead, to one conclusion and then a completely different conclusion is drawn. This fallacy often occurs when, in the course of discussing one issue, an arguer begins to argue about an entirely different (though somehow related) issue. It also occurs when an arguer draws a conclusion that goes far beyond anything for which he or she has provided evidence.

8. The *red herring* fallacy is similar to the fallacy of missing the point. It occurs when an arguer diverts the attention of the reader or listener by going off on extraneous issues and points but ends by assuming that some conclusion relevant to the point at hand has been established. In the red herring fallacy, the argumentation seems to have the purpose of throwing the reader or listener off the right track. In missing the point, the argument points clearly to some conclusion, but that conclusion is not the same as the one at issue; in the red herring fallacy, the argument usually does not point clearly to any conclusion.

Sample Exercises from Exercise 3.2. Part I

1. The position open in the accounting department should be given to Frank Thompson. Frank has six hungry children to feed, and his wife desperately needs an operation to save her eyesight.

    This argument is an appeal to pity. Whether Frank Thompson should be given the open position in the accounting department depends on considerations such as whether he is qualified for such a position, whether he has experience in accounting, and so forth. But the argument simply tries to evoke pity and sympathy for Frank Thompson, and does not address the relevant issues.

2. Publishing magnate Steve Forbes has argued at length that the fairest kind of income tax is a flat tax. But Forbes is a billionaire, and he stands to save millions of dollars if a flat tax is enacted. Therefore, we can hardly take Forbes's arguments seriously.

    This argument is an *ad hominem* fallacy of the circumstantial variety. The arguer tries to discredit whatever points Steve Forbes has made, not by considering the content of these points, but rather only indicating circumstances in which Forbes finds himself, suggesting furtively that Forbes has strong motives for arguing as he does quite irrespective of the truth. The argument is not an *ad hominem* abusive because the arguer does not directly insult Forbes or hurl abusive accusations in his direction.

3. The proposal has been made that we award the prize for best watercolor painting to Cynthia Bradley. But did you hear that Cynthia just had an operation for breast implants? Apparently she thinks that will make her more attractive. She doesn't realize that what

men find most attractive is eyes. Let's see . . . . Why don't we give the prize to Kristie Smith? Her painting is just beautiful.

The fallacy committed here is red herring. The arguer goes wildly off the track chasing the "red herring" of what Cynthia Bradley may think attractive about women to men; then finally the arguer returns from off the track to the topic of who should get the prize for best watercolor, drawing a conclusion without having presented any evidence that is genuinely relevant to this topic.

4. Whoever thrusts a knife into another person should be arrested. But surgeons do precisely this when operating. Therefore, surgeons should be arrested.

This argument commits the fallacy of accident. It begins with a general proposition that has a kind of moral force. Then it concludes to a particular application of this general proposition, while neglecting to consider the special, "accidental" features of this particular application.

Additional Exercises for Section 3.2. Part I

Identify the fallacies of relevance in the following arguments.

1. The rule of a majority, which in any population must be in effect an unorganized and untutored mob, is an obviously undesirable political situation. It follows for this reason that the basic principle of democratic government is refuted.

2. Fifty million Americans have tried Brand X cigarettes. You should try them, too.

3. Most students on this campus are in favor of serving beer at student dining facilities. It follows that this is a good idea.

4. The right to possess property is fundamental. If, then, I should want to purchase an automatic weapon for my own use, I should be allowed to do so.

5. Women are genetically determined to be, on the average, smaller and weaker than men. They are just naturally different. It follows that the whole idea of women occupying combat positions in the military is, in the nature of things, ridiculous.

6. Life is precious; it is really the supreme moral value. So it is clear that abortion is morally wrong.

7. Women certainly have a right to do what they want with their very own bodies. So it is clear that abortion is morally allowable.

8. Vava Voom has been arguing on national television that Americans should send relief packages to starving children in poor countries. But no one should be convinced by her—after all, Miss Voom is nothing but a cheap actress who works in porno films.

9. Republicans have been arguing that massive tax cuts to business and industry are necessary to get the economy back into a healthy state. But in considering their program, just remember that the Republicans are precisely the business people and industrialists who will most immediately benefit from such a tax cut.

28

10. Cast your vote for Yuri Fink for student president. Fink has never won a student election before and feels very depressed about this fact. It would be a great tragedy if he graduated without winning a single campus honor. You can do something about it, now.

11. There can't be anything very wrong with stealing from your employer, since nearly everyone does it.

12. Professor, I need a good grade in this class. If I don't make a 3.0 grade point average, I will lose my scholarship and student offices, and I just don't think I could live under those circumstances.

13. We should not dismiss Mr. Writeoff from the vice-presidency; after all, he was an orphan and has been crippled for several years.

14. If you students don't think you should invite me to the class party, just reflect that I still have not turned in the grades for the class.

15. You should do unto others as you would have them do unto you. Since you are so suicidal, therefore, what you should do is attempt to terminate others' lives.

16. Reflect for a moment that this policy has been the standing policy of the Gestapo since its beginnings, and that its opponents have all, let us say, failed to flourish. Then I know you'll begin to appreciate the wisdom of this policy.

17. Of course gay activists have called for increased research on AIDS. Obviously, the discovery of a vaccine would be to their great advantage. We therefore should discourage such research.

18. You say you object to the American foreign policy in Europe. You ought to go become a citizen of Bosnia then.

19. Gentlemen, the dean has accused our department of irresponsibility in managing our budget. But I happen to know that the dean overspent his own budget this year in every category.

20. Don't be just a face in the crowd. Wear FineFare shirts and jeans.

3.3   FALLACIES OF WEAK INDUCTION

When fallacies of weak induction are committed, the defect in the argument that makes the argument fallacious is not that the premises are logically irrelevant to the conclusion, as with fallacies of relevance. Rather, the defect is that the connection between the premises of argument and its conclusion is not strong enough to make the conclusion very likely or very rational to believe on the basis of the premises. In effect, then, the fallacies of weak induction are weak inductive arguments. Six types will be discussed in this section.

9.   The *appeal to unqualified authority* (*argumentum ad verecundiam*) occurs when an arguer cites the testimony or belief of an authority who is not necessarily reliable or who is not an expert in the subject at hand. Citing a legitimate, reliable authority is not committing this fallacy (although such a citation cannot ever amount to a valid deductive argument).

10.   The *appeal to ignorance* (*argumentum ad ignorantiam*) occurs in an argument when the premises state that nothing is known with certainty about a certain subject, and the conclu-

sion states something definite about that subject. A typical use of the appeal to ignorance is to argue that because a certain thesis has not be proven, the opposite of that thesis must be true. This fallacy is not committed, however, if the premises state that qualified researchers in the subject at hand have failed after extensive attempts to demonstrate something, and the conclusion states that what they have attempted to demonstrate is not so. Also, this fallacy is not committed in the special context of the courtroom, where a defendant is presumed innocent until proven guilty.

11.   The fallacy of *hasty generalization* (*converse accident*) is committed when a conclusion is drawn about all the members of a group or population from premises about some sample of the group that is not representative. A sample is not usually representative if it is too small or is not randomly selected.

12.   The fallacy of *false cause* occurs when the link between premises and conclusion in an argument depends on the supposition of some causal connection that does not in fact exist. One variety of the false cause fallacy occurs when it is concluded that one type of event causes another just because events of the first type are regularly followed by events of the second type. This is called *post hoc ergo propter hoc* ("after this therefore because of this"); an example would be to conclude that my watch's coming around to 5:00 or 6:00 A.M. causes the sun to rise. Another variety of the false cause fallacy, called *non causa pro causa* ("not the cause for the cause"), occurs when something taken to be a cause is not a cause at all and the mistake is based on something other than temporal succession. A third variety of the false cause fallacy we may call *oversimplified cause*. It occurs when two or more causal factors are conjointly responsible for a given effect, but the arguer picks one of these causal factors and presents it as the sole cause of that effect.

13.   The fallacy of *slippery slope* is a variety of the false cause fallacy. It occurs when the conclusion of an argument depends on the claim that a certain event or situation will initiate a more or less long chain of events leading to some undesirable consequence, and when there is not sufficient reason to think that the chain of events will actually take place.

14.   The fallacy of *weak analogy* occurs in inductive arguments from analogy when the analogy between two things is not strong enough to support the conclusion. The basic form of an argument from analogy is

> Entity A has attributes *a, b, c, d*, and *z*.
> Entity B has attributes *a, b, c*, and *d*.
> Therefore, entity B probably has attribute *z*, too.

For this to be a strong inductive argument, there must be some systematic (causal) connection between possession of the attributes *a* through *d* and possession of the attribute *z*. If such a systematic connection does not exist, the argument is weak and commits the fallacy of weak analogy.

Sample Exercises from Exercise 3.3. Part I

1.   The *Daily News* carried an article this morning about three local teenagers who were arrested on charges of drug possession. Teenagers these days are nothing but a bunch of junkies.

This argument commits the fallacy of hasty generalization (converse accident). From evidence cited about three local teenagers, the argument concludes to a generalization about all teenagers these days.

2. If a car breaks down on the freeway, a passing mechanic is not obligated to render emergency road service. For similar reasons, if a person suffers a heart attack on the street, a passing physician is not obligated to render emergency medical assistance.

   This argument is a weak analogy. In some respects the situation of a mechanic rendering emergency road service is the same as the situation of a physician rendering emergency medical assistance. But in several crucial respects—for instance with regard to the possibly life-saving importance of the service rendered—the two situations are different. (The careful student will notice that in this example, moral issues are at stake, and that the inductive character typical of many arguments from analogy is not present here.)

3. There must be something to psychical research. Three famous physicists, Oliver Lodge, James Jeans, and Arthur Stanley Eddington, took it seriously.

   This argument is an appeal to unqualified authority (*ad verecundiam*).

4. The secretaries have asked us to provide lounge areas where they can spend their coffee breaks. This request will have to be refused. If we give them lounge areas, the next thing they'll ask for will be spas and swimming pools. Then it will be racquetball courts, tennis courts, and fitness centers. Expenditures for these facilities will drive us into bankruptcy.

   This argument commits the fallacy of slippery slope. No cogent evidence that the feared chain reaction will occur is provided.

Additional Exercises for Section 3.3

1. Mary must have ESP: last night she had a weird dream about her mother and this morning her mother had a heart attack.

2. Ninety-five percent of heroin addicts smoked marijuana before they became addicted to heroin. It is obvious that marijuana leads to heroin addiction.

3. This logic course has been extraordinarily boring and tedious, so I'll never take another philosophy course again.

4. No less a person than the illustrious General Isa Sidewinder supports this water bond issue. It therefore just has to be the right thing to do to issue these water bonds.

5. No one has found every link in the supposed chain from one-celled animals to human beings. It follows that the theory of evolution is nothing but a myth.

6. The 1960s were the heyday of permissive childrearing in the United States. Today in this country we have the highest crime rate in history, with most of the convicted criminals being in their early and middle twenties. It follows that if we want to prevent the crime rate from going even higher, we must put a stop to the permissive raising of children.

7. After many years of writing philosophy, the philosopher Friedrich Nietzsche went stark raving mad. This fact shows the extremely dangerous nature of the subject of philosophy.

8. No one has ever genuinely seen God or talked with him, despite the lies of the evangelists on television. It follows that God just does not exist.

9. If we adopt the North American Free Trade Agreement, the governments of Central and South America will demand that we buy their goods and hire their nationals in our factories. Soon, American industry will be unable to compete with companies to the

South of our borders. Then our national sovereignty will erode as we become progressively poorer and as the other countries in our hemisphere become progressively richer.

10. Deadly nightshade, mandrake, and belladonna are solanaceous plants and are well-known to be poisonous. It follows that the common tomato, another solanaceous plant, ought to be poisonous as well.

11. If we given in to student demands to deemphasize examinations, pretty soon the students will be demanding that all exams be abolished. Then they'll go on to insist that we turn our universities into nothing but private clubs and health resorts.

12. The large, white mushrooms sold in grocery stores are delicious and healthy to eat. These mushrooms here in the woods are large and white. So they ought to be delicious and healthy, too; let's pick and eat them.

13. The Crash of the stock market in the 1930s was preceded by a decade of rising paper prosperity. Since we have now had a decade of rising paper prosperity, it follows that very likely we are headed for another stock market crash.

14. Since human beings and computers both perform many intelligent functions such as calculating, controlling, and regulating, it follows that we should consider computers to be thinking beings just like ourselves.

15. This survey showed that Americans oppose arms control talks with the Eastern Europeans. It polled a wide range of students at all three of our military academies, and 85 percent of them are against arms control negotiations.

16. The claims of mediums and clairvoyants have never really been completely refuted. It follows therefore that their claims are reasonable to believe.

17. Violent sex offenders have nearly all been consumers of pornographic materials. If we want to reduce violent sex crimes in our country, then we should first make pornographic materials illegal.

18. If you want to know whether the budget deficit is a serious problem or not, just bear this in mind: Leading public figures like Madonna, Michael Jackson, and Chuck Norris have all maintained the seriousness of the deficit.

19. I tried a hamburger at one of Hamburger City's chain of franchised restaurants, and it was terrible. I'll never eat anything at a restaurant in that chain again.

20. If you really want to cure your cold, just take chicken soup and lemon juice for a while. People who do so find their cold cured in about a week.

3.4 FALLACIES OF PRESUMPTION, AMBIGUITY, AND GRAMMATICAL ANALOGY

The *fallacies of presumption* include begging the question, complex question, false dichotomy, and suppressed evidence. In these fallacies, the premises either presume what they purport to show (as with the first two of these fallacies) or else presume distorted versions of the truth (as with the last two of these fallacies).

15. The fallacy of *begging the question* (*petitio principii*) occurs when the arguer uses some trick or device to hide the fact that a premise may not be true. When this fallacy is

committed, the argument must be valid, one premise must be questionable, and some artifice must be employed to hide the questionable status of the premise in question. One typical way of begging the question is simply to leave a crucial premise out of the argument altogether. Another typical way of begging the question is to present a premise that more or less has the same meaning as the conclusion but is worded differently. A third typical way of begging the question is to restate the conclusion as a premise in a long chain of inferences. Begging the question has also been called circular reasoning.

16.   The fallacy of *complex question* occurs when an apparently single question is asked that really involves two or more questions, all of which are answered by any appropriate answer to the apparently single question. Such a question is the familiar "Have you stopped beating your wife?" which involves the two questions "Did you ever beat your wife?" and "If you did ever beat your wife, have you stopped?" The complex question, although not itself an argument, is such that the question, taken together with an answer to it, yields an argument that establishes the truth of some proposition presupposed in the question. Thus, the proposition presupposed in the question "have you stopped beating your wife?" is "You once did beat your wife," and whether the person answers "yes" or "no" to the question the truth of this proposition will be implied.

17.   False Dichotomy. A dichotomy is a pair of alternatives (states, characteristics, or conditions) that are both mutually exclusive and jointly exhaustive. A pair X, Y is mutually exclusive if nothing can be both X and Y; it is jointly exhaustive if everything must be either X or Y. A false dichotomy is a pair of alternatives, presented as if it were a dichotomy when it is not in fact a dichotomy. The *fallacy of false dichotomy* is committed when an argument rests for its goodness on presenting some pair of conditions as if it were a dichotomy when it is not. The usual method is to present a false dichotomy in a premise with the *either . . . or* form, known as a disjunctive premise. The argument then proceeds fallaciously in one of two ways. First, one of the alternatives is denied and the other is concluded to. When the alternatives are not jointly exhaustive (or in other words, when the disjunctive premise is simply not true), this procedure is fallacious, though the argument looks like the valid argument form known as disjunctive syllogism. Second, one of the alternatives is affirmed and the denial of the other is concluded to. When the alternatives are not mutually exclusive, this procedure is fallacious, though the argument looks like a valid argument form using the so-called "exclusive or."

18.   The fallacy of *suppressed evidence* is a fallacy of presumption that is closely related to begging the question. It consists in passing off what are at best half-truths as if they were the whole truth and using them as premises in an argument. This fallacy is also committed if an arguer presents the premises in such a way as to imply that they are the only facts relevant to the conclusion when in fact there are other relevant facts that point in the opposite direction. One example of such a fallacy is, "You ought to become a Hollywood starlet; starlets are so glamorous, they make money easily, and they quickly rise to full-fledged stardom."

The *fallacies of ambiguity* include equivocation and amphiboly. In both cases the faultiness of the argument arises because of some ambiguity in either the premises or conclusion or both.

19.   The fallacy of *equivocation occurs* when the inference in an argument depends on the fact that a word or phrase is used in two or more different senses. For example, "Banks have lots of money in them; the sides of rivers are banks; therefore, the sides of rivers have lots of money in them," is an argument in which the inference depends on the word "banks," which is equivocated upon (used with different senses) in the argument.

20.   The fallacy of *amphiboly* occurs when an arguer, beginning with some statement that is ambiguous owing to its syntactical structure, proceeds to interpret it in a way in which it was

not intended and to draw a conclusion based on this faulty interpretation. The original statement is usually made by someone other than the arguer. The syntactical ambiguity is often due to mistakes in grammar or punctuation, such as dangling modifiers, confusion of restrictive and nonrestrictive clauses and phrases, and ambiguous reference of pronoun to antecedent. A well-known example of amphiboly is Groucho Marx's classic "One morning I shot an elephant in my pajamas. How he got into my pajamas I'll never know."

The main difference between amphiboly and equivocation is that in amphiboly the ambiguity is traceable to syntactical structure in a *statement,* whereas in equivocation the ambiguity is traceable to a *word* that has two or more distinct senses. If the ambiguity in an argument can be removed by a syntactical or grammatical alteration, such as a change in punctuation or a rearrangement of words, it is an amphiboly. If the ambiguity is removable only by a substitution of different terms, it is probably an equivocation.

The *fallacies of grammatical analogy* include composition and division. In these fallacies arguments are employed that, though faulty, are grammatically analogous to other arguments that are unimpeachable. The similarity in linguistic structure makes the fallacious argument appear good. In composition and division the faultiness in the argument arises because an attribute or characteristic is improperly transferred from parts of a whole to the whole or from the whole itself to its parts. The whole in question might be a physical whole composed of physical parts, a class composed of members, or a species composed of the entities it comprises. Of special relevance to the fallacies of grammatical analogy is the difference between *distributive* and *collective* predication of an attribute. An attribute is predicated distributively if it is meant to apply to each and every one of the members of the group. An attribute is predicated collectively if it is meant to apply to the group taken as a whole. "Whooping cranes are scarce" is, for example, a collective predication—it does not mean that each whopping crane is scarce. Shifting illegitimately between distributive and collective predications of an attribute is one form of the fallacies of grammatical analogy.

21.   The fallacy of *composition* occurs when the inference in an argument depends on the erroneous transference of a characteristic from the parts of something to the whole. For instance, going from a distributive predication to the corresponding collective predication is one sort of fallacy of composition. Another would be going from the characteristics of the elements of a chemical compound to the characteristics of the compound ("Hydrogen and oxygen are gases; therefore, H_2O is a gas"). Not every instance of transferring characteristics from parts to wholes is illegitimate, so not every instance of such transference is a fallacy of composition.

22.   The fallacy of *division* occurs when the inference in an argument depends on the erroneous transference of a characteristic from a whole to some one or more of its parts. Division is the exact reverse of composition.

Composition and division are sometimes confused with hasty generalization and accident, respectively. Composition can be distinguished from hasty generalization as follows: in hasty generalization, the conclusion is not an assertion about a group taken as a whole (a collective predication); rather, it is an assertion about all (each and every one of) the members of a group (a distributive predication). But in composition the assertion in the conclusion is a collective predication. Similarly, division can be distinguished from accident as follows: in accident the inference is from a general assertion (a distributive predication) to a specific assertion, but in division the inference is from an assertion about a group taken as a whole (a collective predication) to an assertion about the members of the group.

Sample Exercises for Exercise 3.4. Part I

1. Either we require forced sterilization of third world peoples or world population will explode and all of us will die. We certainly don't want to die, so we must require forced sterilization.

   This argument commits the fallacy of false dichotomy. A possibility that is excluded without evidence by the dichotomy in the first premise of this argument is the possibility that, even without forced sterilization of third world peoples, we avoid a world population explosion and the death of us all.

2. Every sentence in this paragraph is well written. Therefore, the paragraph is well written.

   This argument is a fallacy of composition. It moves illegitimately from an attribution of a characteristic to all the parts of a whole thing to an attribution of the characteristic to the whole thing itself.

3. An athlete is a human being. Therefore, a good athlete is a good human being.

   This argument commits the fallacy of equivocation. The equivocation is on the word "good." A good salesman is a salesman who sells large quantities; but a good human being is a morally admirable one.

4. James said that he saw a picture of a beautiful girl stashed in Stephen's locker. We can only conclude that Stephen has broken the rules, because girls are not allowed in the locker room.

   This argument commits the fallacy of amphiboly. The crucial ambiguity is that concerning whether the phrase "stashed in Stephen's locker" applies to the picture or to the girl. Very likely the premise requires for its truth that the phrase apply to the picture. But the conclusion requires for its cogency that the phrase applies to the girl.

Additional Exercises for Section 3.4

Identify the fallacies of presupposition, ambiguity, and grammatical analogy in the following arguments.

1. Almost every person in the U.S. has two arms. That alone shows the tremendous need for gun control laws in this country.

2. Weeds are plentiful this year. Therefore, this particular dandelion is plentiful this year.

3. Children should be seen and not heard. This is obvious because only adults should be both seen and heard.

4. The news said that, waving majestically in the breeze, Victoria saw the Stars and Stripes. I wonder if she would notice the flag if she stopped behaving so haughtily.

5. The report said that, stepping up to the podium, John cleared his throat and delivered a two-hour extemporaneous address. It must have taken John a long time to step up to that podium.

6. *Al:* Do you make a lot of profit on your narcotics sales?
   Betty: No!
   Al: So you do indeed sell narcotics.

7. *Political ad:* You can either vote for me or else commit this nation to slavery at the hands of the Communists by 1995.

8. *News item:* The stealthy reconnaissance agent spied the giant Russian weapons factory hiding in a small clump of grass.
   Reader: Those Russians really are advanced, getting that entire factory hidden in that grass.

9. *Sign:* East at Sloppy Joe's and you'll never eat anyplace else again.
   Patron: Sloppy Joe must be seasoning his burgers with arsenic these days.

10. Joe told his worst enemy, Sam, that he was a swine. Joe must have a lot of character to make an admission like that to his own worst enemy.

11. John sat absolutely glued to his seat during the movie. He must have had a lot of trouble getting unstuck when the show ended.

12. Auto thefts are occurring at an alarming rate this month. It must be technology that is enabling thieves to carry out such speedy robberies.

13. It says here on the sports page that the Boosters' Club had seasoned Coach Passa Bomb at its annual awards banquet. It looks like cannibalism has finally broken out openly among the boosters.

14. I've heard that 55 percent of all Americans are fat. But that can't be right: I'm sure that no more than 40 percent of me is fat.

15. A cat or dog has the attribute of normalcy only if it has four legs. It follows that a bird or a man has the property of normalcy only if it has four legs.

16. All pieces of chalk are white. It follows that the class of all pieces of chalk is white.

17. John said that he smoked his pipes and listened with both ears. John must have looked pretty strange with those pipes in his ears.

18. The real numbers are continuous, and the number one is a real number. So the number one is continuous.

19. Strauss's tunes are very light, so probably even a little child could carry them.

20. Cells are tiny. An elephant is nothing but cells. So an elephant is tiny.

3.5 FALLACIES IN ORDINARY LANGUAGE

The student should bear in mind that the twenty-two fallacies that have been discussed have been presented as if they occurred isolated from one another, as "pure" and fairly clear cases; whereas in argumentation the student will most often encounter in everyday life, fallacies do not typically occur in isolation from one another or in clearly identifiable ways. Often in everyday argumentation, fallacies occur combined with one another, clothed in various emotional ornamentations, and obscured by unclear lines of argumentative development.

In sorting out the logic of ordinary argumentation, the student will need to bring to bear all the resources of logical analysis, at least in the typical cases. Knowledge of meaning, knowledge of difference between deduction and induction as well as the kinds of excellence and deficiency belonging to each kind of argument, and knowledge of typically fallacious forms of argumentation are necessary. There is no clear-cut guaranteed method by which absolutely every argument may be completely appraised logically. The information so far presented is indispensable, but in order to protect oneself from fallacious argumentation one must always think carefully before giving one's assent.

Additional Exercises for Section 3.5

Identify the fallacy or fallacies in the following arguments.

1. If we do not match the Japanese product for product, their economic adventurism will soon spread from Asia to the Middle East. Eventually we'll lose control of our home markets and our entire economy will collapse.

2. The Roman Empire, poised at the height of its power but eaten up by internal moral decay, had only a few years of political integrity left to it, though none of its contemporary citizens realized that gloomy fact. The moral for our nation is obvious.

3. Today's youth are callow and insensitive. Why, my Aunt Emma has spent years trying to get the young people of her neighborhood interested in proper diet. She marches up and down the street handing out, free mind you, dietary plans to any teenager who will take them. But do you think they are interested? They just stuff their faces with cola and chips and go on their way.

4. Auto racing is the sport for you. It's fun, it's challenging, and it's exciting.

5. I don't know why people still bring up the subject of Hiroshima. We dropped a bomb, and it destroyed some buildings and killed some people. But that's to be expected in a war.

6. This animal has four legs, hair, and a tail. Therefore, we can reasonably expect that it will have a diet similar to that of a horse.

7. At LeMon Auto Sales every used car on our lot has been individually inspected by Mr. LeMon himself. He makes sure that every car we offer to the public meets his own personal standards. That's why it makes good sense to buy a LeMon.

8. Unless we maintain severe penalties for possession of small amounts of marijuana, it's inevitable that penalties for possession of large amounts of the drug will eventually be lowered. After that, the penalties for possessing hard drugs will become lighter. We can expect that hallucinogens and opiates will become as common on our streets as candy.

9. The universe is like a giant organism, with parts mutually interlocking like tissues and organs. We may conclude, then, that its origin is biological and begin our search for its parents.

10. A household that fails to maintain a balanced budget will eventually go bankrupt. Now consider a government that has a consistent policy of deficit spending, maintained over many years. Like the household, it must eventually go bankrupt.

11. Just allow prosecutors to reintroduce evidence obtained via a technical error in procedure, and pretty soon judges will be allowing evidence obtained via substantial illegality in conduct. Then the entire Fourth Amendment will be rendered in effect null and void.

12. Coeducational dormitories must be stopped at all costs. No parent wants to send a son or daughter to school and have that son or daughter forced to submit to the invasion of every aspect of privacy.

13. It's obvious that the educational philosophy of our decade has gone astray. Students are late to classes, they have no sense of discipline, and they like blue jeans and T-shirts better than coats and ties. Why, today people don't even care enough about our educational programs to attend PTA meetings. If a student is spanked, some lawyer immediately hauls a teacher into court. Lawyers are much too powerful anyway.

14. There can be no doubt that communists are infiltrating everywhere. Even the local public library recently sponsored an evening lecture on transcendental meditation. Women's-rights activists hand out fliers in one of our local shopping malls, and the Branch Davidians solicit donations at the airport. I don't know why we tolerate this sort of thing. The city council should levy a fine against all public loiterers. The city council has been so ineffective in recent years. The weak city council is the basic reason for the spread of communism in our city.

15. The objective historian must admit that Adolf Hitler was an admirable national leader. He solved Germany's economic problems, he restored the patriotic pride of nearly every German citizen, and he reinstituted order and discipline in public life. He made Germany into a nation that other nations could ignore no longer.

16. Football must go at this university. The student body just cannot tolerate these recruiting scandals and the extra privileges accorded to scholarship athletes.

17. Soccer and football are both played on a large field with a ball that is often kicked in the course of the game. It follows that the typical good football player would make a good soccer player.

18. My last cocker spaniel was a parti-colored female and she was an excellent hunter. It follows that this parti-colored cocker female will be an excellent hunter, too.

19. I bought XYZ stock last year after a long decline in the market, and made a nice profit on it when the market went back up. So, since the market has again been on a long decline, I ought to by XYZ stock again.

20. A guest-worker program for foreign nationals would be a disaster for this country. Every country in the world would have its citizens clamoring for admission to the U.S.A. The prospect of paying them cheap wages would encourage businesses to entice them here. Foreign nationals would collect in ghettos, and pretty soon we would have pockets of foreigners in our midst, speaking their own languages and practicing their own customs. These would become pockets of crime and the victim would be the average law-abiding U.S. citizen.

4

CATEGORICAL
PROPOSITIONS

4.1   THE COMPONENTS OF CATEGORICAL PROPOSITIONS

A *categorical proposition* is a proposition that relates two classes, or categories, denoted respectively by the *subject term* and the *predicate term*. The categorical proposition asserts that either all or part of the class denoted by the subject term is either included in or excluded from the class denoted by the predicate term. There are thus four basic types of categorical proposition, and each type can be put into one of the following four *standard forms:*

> All *S* are *P*.
> No *S* are *P*.
> Some *S* are *P*.
> Some *S* are not *P*.

In these standard forms, *S* stands for the subject term and *P* for the predicate term. The words "all," "no," and "some" are called logical *quantifiers*. (Note that "some" is understood to have the meaning "at least one.") The words "are" and "are not" are called *copulas*.

Sample Exercises from Exercise 4.1

1. Some college students are avid devotees of soap operas.

quantifier:	Some
subject term:	college students
copula:	are
predicate term:	avid devotees of soap operas

2. No persons who live near airports are persons who appreciate the noise of jets.

quantifier:	No
subject term:	persons who live near airports
copula:	are
predicate term:	persons who appreciate the noise of jets

3. All oil-based paints are products that contribute significantly to photochemical smog.

quantifier:	All
subject term:	oil-based paints
copula:	are
predicate term:	products that contribute significantly to photochemical smog

4. Some preachers who are intolerant of others' beliefs are not television evangelists.

quantifier:	Some
subject term:	preachers who are intolerant of others' beliefs
copula:	are not
predicate term:	television evangelists

4.2   QUALITY, QUANTITY, AND DISTRIBUTION

In class notation "All *S* are *P*" means that every member of the *S* class is a member of the *P* class. "No *S* are *P*" means that no member of the *S* class is a member of the *P* class. "Some *S* are *P*" means that at least one member of the *S* class is a member of the *P* class. "Some *S* are not *P*" means that at least one member of the *S* class is not a member of the *P* class. The *quality* of a categorical proposition is defined as *affirmative* if it affirms class membership (as do "All *S* are *P*" and "Some *S* are *P*") and *negative* if it denies class membership (as do "No *S* are *P*" and "Some *S* are not *P*"). The *quantity* of a categorical proposition is defined as *universal* if it makes a claim about every member of the *S* class (as do "All *S* are *P*" and "No *S* are *P*") and *particular* if it makes a claim about just some (at least one) member of the *S* class (as do "Some *S* are *P*" and "Some *S* are not *P*").

The universal affirmative categorical proposition ("All *S* are *P*") is known as an **A** proposition; the universal negative categorical proposition ("No *S* are *P*") is known as an **E** proposition; the particular affirmative categorical proposition ("Some *S* are *P*") is known as an **I** proposition; and the particular negative categorical proposition ("Some *S* are not *P*") is known as an **O** proposition.

The *distribution* of a term (either *S* or *P*) in a categorical proposition is follows. A term is *distributed* in a proposition if and only if that proposition makes a claim about every member of the class denoted by that term; otherwise, the term is *undistributed* in the proposition. Clearly the *S* term in an **A** proposition is distributed. The *P* term in an **A** proposition is undistributed. In an **E** proposition both the *S* term and the *P* term are distributed. In an **I** proposition both the *S* term and the *P* term are undistributed. In an **O** proposition the *S* term is undistributed, but the *P* term is distributed.

The following two mnemonic sentences should help students remember the correct pattern of distribution of terms. First, "**U**nprepared **S**tudents **N**ever **P**ass" reminds us that **U**niversals distribute **S**ubjects, and **N**egatives distribute **P**redicates. Second, the sentence "**A**ny **S**tudent **E**arning **B**s **I**s **N**ot **O**n **P**robation" indicates that in the **A** proposition the **S** (subject) term is distributed; in the **E** proposition **B**oth subject and predicate terms are distributed; in the **I** proposition **N**either (subject nor predicate) term is distributed; and in the **O** proposition the **P** (predicate) term is distributed.

The material of this section may be summarized in the following table:

Proposition letter	Quality	Quantity	Terms distributed
A	affirmative	universal	*S*
E	negative	universal	*S* and *P*
I	affirmative	particular	None
O	negative	particular	*P*

40

1. No mobsters are persons who make good Labor Secretaries.

letter name:	**E**
quantity:	universal
quality:	negative
subject term:	mobsters (distributed)
predicate term:	persons who make good Labor Secretaries (distributed)

2. All governments that bargain with terrorists are governments that encourage terrorism.

letter name:	**A**
quantity:	universal
quality:	affirmative
subject term:	governments that bargain with terrorists (distributed)
predicate term:	governments that encourage terrorism (undistributed)

3. Some symphony orchestras are organizations on the brink of bankruptcy.

letter name:	**I**
quantity:	particular
quality:	affirmative
subject term:	symphony orchestras (undistributed)
predicate term:	organizations on the brink of bankruptcy (undistributed)

4. Some Chinese leaders are not thoroughgoing opponents of capitalist economics.

letter name:	**O**
quantity:	particular
quality:	negative
subject term:	Chinese leaders (undistributed)
predicate term:	thoroughgoing opponents of capitalist economics (distributed)

4.3 VENN DIAGRAMS AND THE MODERN SQUARE OF OPPOSITION

An ambiguity exists in the meaning of the **A**-type proposition "All S are P," and in the meaning of the **E**-type proposition "No S are P." If these propositions are taken to imply the existence of at least one member of the class denoted by their subject term "S," and their predicate term "P," then the propositions are being understood in the *traditional* or *Aristotelian* sense. But if these propositions are not taken to imply the existence of at least one member of the class denoted by their subject term "S," and of at least one member of the class denoted by their predicate term "P," then the propositions are being understood in the *modern* or *Boolean* sense.

On the modern interpretation, the **A**-type proposition "All S are P," is understood to mean "There does not exist an S that fails to be a P." Clearly, if there is no S at all, then there is no S that fails to be P, so that the **A**-proposition is true in this case.

Similarly, on the modern interpretation, the **E**-type proposition "No S are P," is understood to mean "There does not exist an S that is a P." Clearly, if there is no S at all, then there is no S that is a P, so that the **E**-proposition is true in this case.

Thus, on the modern interpretation of the **A**-type proposition and of the **E**-type proposition, if there is no S at all, then both the **A**-type and the **E**-type propositions are true.

The following summarizes the modern interpretation of all of the categorical propositions:

A = "All S are P" = There does not exist an S that fails to be a P.
I = "Some S are P" = There does exist an S that is a P.
E = "No S are P" = There does not exist an S that is a P.
O = "Some S are not P" = There does exist an S that fails to be a P.

In the nineteenth century, the economist and logician John Venn invented a diagrammatic manner of representing the four categorical propositions in their modern interpretation. With the summary just given of the modern interpretation of the categorical propositions in mind, we should find fairly self-explanatory the following account of Venn's diagrammatic representations, known as *Venn Diagrams*

Venn diagrams are ways of pictorially representing the informational content of categorical propositions. The basic conventions for such diagrams are as follows:

1. Each term is represented by a circle. (When two terms are involved, the diagram contains two overlapping circles, one for each term.)

2. The area inside the circle for a term represents the extension of that term, and the area outside the circle represents everything not in the extension of that term.

3. The areas of overlap and nonoverlap of the circles represent things in an obvious way, given convention (2). Thus, for example, the football-shaped region of overlap between the two circles represents things that are in both the extensions of the two terms involved.

4. Shading of an area means that the class of things represented by that area is empty; placing an "X" in an area indicates that the correlated class is not empty—that is, that there is at least one thing in it.

5. If a given area is neither shaded out nor filled in with an "X," nothing is said about the corresponding class.

Using Venn diagrams, we may conveniently represent all four of the categorical propositions in their modern interpretations. The **A** proposition may be represented by

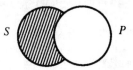

The **E** proposition may be represented by

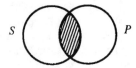

The **I** proposition may be represented by

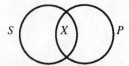

The **O** proposition may be represented by

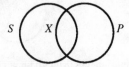

The diagrams show what we noted earlier: that the **A** and **E** propositions in their modern interpretations say nothing at all about the existence of anything.

From the summary previously given of the modern interpretation of the categorical propositions, we can see that the **A**-type and the **O**-type propositions assert the exact opposite of each other. We may also see this fact from the Venn Diagrams for the **A**-type and the **O**-type propositions. The relation between the two types of propositions is said to be the relation of *contradictoriness*. Another way to express that two propositions, like the **A** and the **O**, are contradictory is to say that it cannot be the case that both propositions are true and it cannot be the case that both propositions are false.

From either the summary or the Venn Diagrams, we may see that the **E**-type and the **I**-type propositions assert the exact opposite of each other. Thus, they too are in the relation of contradictoriness.

The double relation of contradictoriness between the **A** and the **O** on the one hand and between the **E** and the **I** on the other, can be represented in a square diagram known as the *modern square of opposition.*

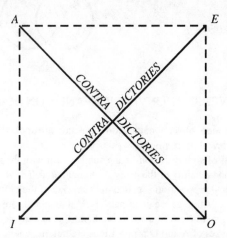

The modern square of opposition helps us deal quickly with certain kinds of inferences involving categorical propositions. These kinds are inferences having a single categorical proposition as sole premise, and a related categorical proposition as conclusion. Such inference are called *immediate inferences*. For example, the modern square tells us that from the truth of an **A**-type proposition we may immediately infer the falsity of the corresponding **O**-type proposition, but we may not immediately infer either the truth or falsity of the corresponding **E**-type proposition or the truth or falsity of the corresponding **I**-type proposition.

Sample Exercises from Exercise 4.3

1. No life decisions are happenings based solely on logic.

   Modern interpretation:

2. All electric motors are machines that depend on magnetism.

   Modern interpretation:

3. Some political campaigns are mere attempts to discredit opponents.

   Modern interpretation:

   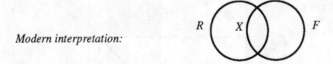

4. Some rock music lovers are not fans of Madonna.

   Modern interpretation:

4.4   CONVERSION, OBVERSION, AND CONTRAPOSITION

The operations of conversion, obversion, and contraposition are applied to categorical propositions to yield new categorical propositions.

   Conversion consists of simply switching the subject term with the predicate term while leaving the quality and the quantity of the proposition unaltered. The result of applying conversion to a categorical proposition is called the *converse* of the proposition. Thus, for example, the converse of "All dogs are mammals" is "All mammals are dogs." The converses of **E** and **I** propositions are *logically equivalent* to them (that is, they necessarily have the same truth values). The converses of **A** and **O** propositions are not, in general, logically equivalent to them.* Similarly, if we form an argument whose premise is a categorical proposition and whose conclusion is the converse of it, then the argument is valid if the premise is an **E** or an **I**

---

*An exception to this point occurs if the *S* term and the *P* term are the same, or are synonymous.

proposition and, in general, is invalid if the premise is an **A** or an **O** proposition. (In the latter case the argument commits the fallacy of *illicit conversion*.)

Obversion consists of both (1) changing the quality of the proposition (leaving the quantity the same), and (2) negating the predicate term. To negate the predicate term, one typically attaches the prefix "non-" to it. The result of obversion is called the *obverse* of the proposition to which it is applied. The obverse of any categorical proposition, **A**, **E**, **I**, or **O**, is logically equivalent to it. Any argument whose premise is a categorical proposition and whose conclusion is its obverse is a valid argument.

Contraposition consists of both (1) switching the subject term with the predicate term (while leaving the quality and quantity of the proposition unaltered), and (2) complementing both terms. Thus, for example, the contrapositive of "All dogs are mammals" is "All non-mammals are non-dogs." The result of contraposition is called the *contrapositive* of the proposition to which it is applied. The contrapositives of **A** propositions and **O** propositions are logically equivalent to the originals, while the contrapositives of **E** and **I** propositions are not, in general, logically equivalent to the originals. If we form an argument whose premise is a categorical proposition and whose conclusion is the contrapositive of it, then the argument is valid if the premise is an **A** or an **O** proposition and, in general, is invalid if the premise is an **E** or an **I** proposition. (In the latter case the argument commits the fallacy of *illicit contraposition*.)

Conversion, obversion, and contraposition may be used in sequence to prove certain arguments valid. There are two basic points to remember. The first is that doubly complementing a term (e.g., non-non-*P*) yields the equivalent of the term that is doubly complemented. The second is that the operations of conversion and contraposition must be correctly applied: conversion must be applied only to **E** and **I** propositions and contraposition only to **A** and **O** propositions. Here is an example of using the operations to show that "All *A* are non-*B*; therefore, no *B* are *A*" is a valid argument:

All *A* are non-*B*.	
All non-non-*B* are non-*A*.	*contraposition of an A proposition*
All *B* are non-*A*.	*replacing "non-non-B" by "B"*
No *B* are non-non-*A*.	obversion
No *B* are *A*.	*replacing "non-non-A" by "A"*

Sample Exercises from Exercise 4.4. Part II

1. a. All homes contaminated by radon gas are potential causes of lung cancer.

    Converse: All potential causes of lung cancer are homes contaminated by radon gas.

    These are *not* logically equivalent.

    b. No sex-change operations are completely successful events.

    Converse: No completely successful events are sex-change operations.

    These *are* logically equivalent.

    c. Some murals by Diego Rivera are works that celebrate the revolutionary spirit.

    Converse: Some works that celebrate the revolutionary spirit are murals by Diego Rivera.

    These *are* logically equivalent.

d. Some forms of carbon are not substances with a crystalline structure.

Converse: Some substances with a crystalline structure are not forms of carbon.

These *are* logically equivalent.

2. a. All radically egalitarian societies are societies that do not preserve individual liberties.

Obverse: No radically egalitarian societies are non-(societies that do not preserve individual liberties).

or: No radically egalitarian societies are societies that preserve individual liberties.

These *are* logically equivalent.

b. No cult leaders are people who fail to brainwash their followers.

Obverse: All cult leaders are non-(people who fail to brainwash their followers).

or: All cult leaders are people who brainwash their followers.

These *are* logically equivalent.

c. Some college football coaches are persons who do not slip money to their players.

Obverse: Some college football coaches are not non-(persons who do not slip money to their players).

or: Some college football coaches are not persons who slip money to their players.

These *are* logically equivalent.

d. Some budgetary cutbacks are not actions fair to the poor.

Obverse: Some budgetary cutbacks are non-(actions fair to the poor).

or: Some budgetary cutbacks are actions unfair to the poor.

These *are* logically equivalent.

Additional Exercises for Section 4.4

Construct the indicated propositions.

1. The obverse of: Some fish are not bass.

2. The contrapositive of: All angels are principalities.

3. The converse of: All ants are non-butterflies.

4. The obverse of the converse of: No mortals are perfect things.

5. The contrapositive of the obverse of: Some dogs are not cats.

6. The converse of the contrapositive of: No gods are idols.

7. The obverse of the contrapositive of the converse of: All wives are workers.

8. The converse of the contrapositive of the obverse of: No insects are non-spiders.

9. The contrapositive of the obverse of the converse of: Some poets are non-authors.

10. The converse of the obverse of the contrapositive of: some wolves are not non-females.

4.5   THE TRADITIONAL SQUARE OF OPPOSITION

The *traditional square of opposition* is, like the modern square of opposition, a square diagram in which logical relations among the **A, I, E,** and **O** propositions are represented. Like the modern square of opposition, the traditional square contains a representation of the relation of contradictoriness that obtains between the **A** and **O** propositions on the one hand and also between the **E** and **I** propositions on the other.

   The traditional square differs from the modern square, however, in that in the traditional square the interpretation adopted of the universal propositions, that is of the **A** proposition "All S are P" and of the **E** proposition "No S are P," is the traditional or Aristotelian interpretation rather than the modern or Boolean interpretation. Recall that according to the traditional interpretation, these propositions are taken to imply the existence of at least one member of the class denoted by their subject term "S." Accordingly, the traditional square of opposition contains representations of logical relations additional to those represented in the modern square.

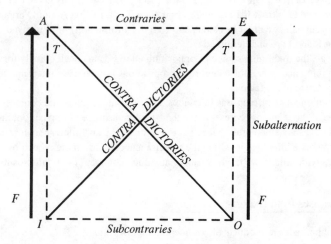

   In order to understand the traditional square, we need to understand the logical relations represented in it. We begin with a review of the relation of contradictoriness and then proceed to the other relations.

   Two propositions are *contradictory* if they cannot both be true and cannot both be false. In other words, they must have opposite truth values—it must be the case that exactly one of them is true and the other false. The **A** and **O** propositions are contradictory, and the **E** and **I** propositions are contradictory.

Two propositions are *contrary* if they cannot both be true but they might both be false. In other words, at least one of them must be false, and possibly both are false. On the traditional interpretation, the **A** and **E** propositions are contrary.

Two propositions are *subcontrary* if they cannot both be false but they might both be true. In other words, at least one of them must be true, and possibly both are true. On the traditional interpretation, the **I** and **O** propositions are subcontrary.

On the traditional interpretation, the **A** and the **I** propositions are related by the logical relation of *subalternation.* This fact means that, traditionally, from the truth of the **A** proposition the truth of the corresponding **I** proposition may be inferred. It also means that, traditionally, from the falsity of the **I** proposition the falsity of the **A** proposition may be inferred. The reverse inferences, however, namely from the truth of **I** to the truth of **A** and from the falsity of **A** to the falsity of **I**, are invalid.

Likewise, on the traditional interpretation, the **E** and the **O** propositions are related by *subalternation.* Thus, traditionally, from the truth of the **E** proposition the truth of the corresponding **O** proposition may be inferred and from the falsity of the **O** proposition the falsity of the **E** proposition may be inferred. The reverse inferences, however, namely from the truth of **O** to the truth of **E** and from the falsity of **E** to the falsity of **O**, are invalid.

As we have just seen, on the traditional interpretation of the categorical propositions, the truth or falsity of one of the categorical propositions often determines the truth or falsity of one or more of the remaining corresponding (that is, having the same subject term and the same predicate term) categorical propositions. The traditional square of opposition allows such determinations to be made quickly. Thus, from the traditional square we can quickly grasp such facts as the following ones.

If **A** is given as false, then **O** is true, but **E** and **I** are undetermined. If **E** is given as false, then **I** is true, but **A** and **O** are undetermined. If **I** is given as false, then **A** is false, **E** is true, and **O** is true. If **O** is given as false, then **A** is true, **E** is false, and **I** is true.

If **A** is given as true, then **E** is false, **I** is true, and **O** is false. If E is given as true, then A is false, I is false, and **O** is true. If **I** is given as true, then **E** is false, but **A** and **O** are undetermined (that is, their truth values cannot be calculated from the information). If **O** is given as true, then **A** is false, but **E** and **I** are undetermined.

In this way, the traditional square of opposition allows us to check quickly for the validity of immediate inferences when the categorical propositions involved are interpreted in the traditional, or Aristotelian, fashion.

When an immediate inference is fallacious, and when its premise and conclusion are related by one of the relations represented in the traditional square of opposition; then the fallacious inference is named after that relation. For example, an "illicit subcontrary" is a fallacious immediate inference in which the premise and conclusion are related by the relation of subcontrariety. Similarly we might speak of an "illicit contrary" or an "illicit subalternation."

Sample Exercises from Exercise 4.5. Part I

1. All fashion fads are products of commercial brainwashing.

   This proposition is given as *true*. It is an **A** proposition. Thus:

   a. "No fashion fads are products of commercial brainwashing" is the corresponding **E** proposition and is false.
   b. "Some fashion fads are products of commercial brainwashing" is the corresponding **I** proposition and is true.

c.   "Some fashion fads are not products of commercial brainwashing" is the corresponding **O** proposition and is false.

2.   All fashion fads are products of commercial brainwashing.

This proposition is given as *false*. It is an **A** proposition. Thus:

a.   "No fashion fads are products of commercial brainwashing" is the corresponding **E** proposition and is undetermined.

b.   "Some fashion fads are products of commercial brainwashing" is the corresponding **I** proposition and is undetermined.

c.   "Some fashion fads are not products of commercial brainwashing" is the corresponding **O** proposition and is true.

3.   No sting operations are cases of entrapment.

This proposition is given as *true*. It is an **E** proposition. Thus:

a.   "All sting operations are cases of entrapment" is the corresponding **A** proposition and is false.

b.   "Some sting operations are cases of entrapment" is the corresponding **I** proposition and is false.

c.   "Some sting operations are not cases of entrapment" is the corresponding **O** proposition and is true.

4.   No sting operations are cases of entrapment.

This proposition is given as *false*. It is an **E** proposition. Thus:

a.   "All sting operations are cases of entrapment" is the corresponding **A** proposition and is undetermined.

b.   "Some sting operations are cases of entrapment" is the corresponding **I** proposition and is true.

c.   "Some sting operations are not cases of entrapment" is the corresponding **O** proposition and is undetermined.

Additional Exercises for Section 4.5

For each of the following specifications of the *S* term and the *P* term, construct the categorical proposition of the indicated type. Tell whether it is true or false. Then, on the basis of this knowledge and nothing else except the logical relations on the traditional square of opposition, tell whether the other three corresponding categorical propositions are true, false, or undetermined.

1.   **A** proposition with *S* = men and *P* = mortals.
2.   **O** proposition with *S* = fish and *P* = bass.
3.   **E** proposition with *S* = dogs and *P* = cats.
4.   **I** proposition with *S* = chairs and *P* = antiques.
5.   **O** proposition with *S* = grasshoppers and *P* = insects.
6.   **A** proposition with *S* = numbers and *P* = even numbers.

7. **E** proposition with S = authors and P = poets.

8. **I** proposition with S = horses and P = palominos.

9. **E** proposition with S = roses and P = plants.

10. **O** proposition with S = elms and P = trees.

4.6   VENN DIAGRAMS AND THE TRADITIONAL STANDPOINT

With minor modifications, Venn diagrams can be used to represent the contents of categorical propositions regarded from the traditional (Aristotelian) standpoint. Thus, with such modifications, Venn diagrams may be used for such tasks as verifying the relationships specified on the traditional square of opposition and to test for the validity of immediate inferences as regarded from the traditional standpoint.

The minor modifications in question concern only the universal propositions (**A** and **E**), because the traditional interpretation and the modern (Boolean) interpretation of the particular propositions (**I** and **O**) are the same. To represent the existential presupposition of the traditional standpoint for the **A** and **E** propositions, we use a capital letter "X" with a circle drawn around it. Thus, the Venn diagrams for the **A**, **E**, **I**, and **O** propositions, interpreted in the traditional (Aristotelian) fashion, follow.

The **A** proposition may be represented by

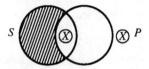

And the **E** proposition may be represented by

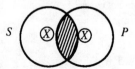

The **I** proposition may be represented by

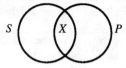

The **O** proposition may be represented by

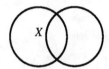

50

The Venn diagram test for the validity of inferences, understood from the traditional standpoint, works in the same way that it does for the modern (Boolean) interpretation. One first diagrams the information of the premise or premises. One then looks at the result to see whether in it the information of the conclusion is represented. If this information is represented then the argument is valid; if this information is not represented then the argument is invalid. One must bear in mind, however, that always if an inference is valid from the Boolean standpoint, then it is valid from the traditional viewpoint (though not necessarily vice versa).

An additional issue arises, however, in evaluating arguments from the traditional point of view: namely, the issue of whether or not in a particular case the use of the traditional point of view is warranted. This issue depends on whether or not things of the sort referred to by the subject terms of the propositions involved actually do exist.

If a Venn diagram test shows the argument being tested to be invalid on the Boolean interpretation but valid on the traditional interpretation; but if the existential presupposition of the traditional viewpoint is not warranted; then we say that the argument is invalid because it commits the "existential fallacy."

In the special case of inferences that involve no alteration of terms between the premise or premises and the conclusion, we may use a *simplified* Venn diagram for the **A** and **E** propositions rather than the *generalized* Venn diagrams that have just been presented. In the simplified Venn diagrams only one of the two circled "X"s is diagrammed; the other is eliminated. The simplified diagrams for the **A** and **E** propositions work as follows.

The **A** proposition is represented by

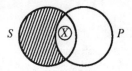

And the **E** proposition is represented by

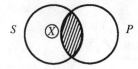

Sample Exercises from Exercise 4.6. Part I:

1. No summer romances are banal pastimes.

   Therefore, it is false that some summer romances are banal pastimes.

   Boolean interpretation:

   Premise:

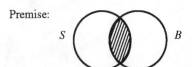

51

Conclusion:

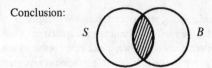

This argument is valid from both the Boolean and the Aristotelian interpretations.

2. It is false that some people who hunger for wealth are not victims of their obsession.

Therefore, some people who hunger for wealth are victims of their obsession.

Boolean interpretation:

Premise:

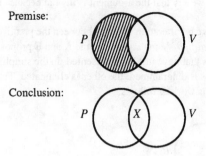

Conclusion:

This argument is invalid from the Boolean standpoint.

Aristotelian interpretation:

Premise:

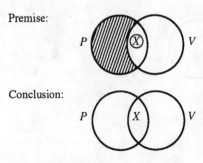

Conclusion:

This argument is valid from the traditional standpoint.

Now, because there do exist people who hunger for wealth, we are warranted in using the traditional interpretation and in regarding this inference as valid.

4.7   TRANSLATING ORDINARY LANGUAGE STATEMENTS
INTO CATEGORICAL FORM

Many statements of ordinary life are not, strictly speaking, categorical propositions. Yet their informational content is that of categorical propositions. In order to make such statements amenable to logical analysis after the patterns developed in Chapter 4, it is necessary to translate them into explicit categorical propositions. The following ten rules of thumb facilitate this task. Nevertheless, no set rules can cover every conceivable case. One must understand the *meaning* of a given statement and then reexpress that meaning, if doing so is possible, as a categorical proposition.

1.   The subject and predicate terms of a categorical proposition must be *nouns* or noun substitutes. If a term in a statement is not a noun, it often may be converted into one. For example, adjectives may be nominalized by adding the word "things" to them. Thus, "All pieces of lead are heavy" may be reexpressed as "All pieces of lead are heavy things."

2.   The copula of a categorical proposition must be "are" or "are not." If the *verb* in a statement is not of this sort, it may often be converted. For example: "Some dogs run fast" may be reexpressed as "Some dogs are fast runners."

3.   Categorical propositions must begin with the quantifiers "no," "some," or "all." If a statement does not start this way, it may often be converted. For instance, *singular propositions* (those about one specific thing) may be reexpressed as universal categorical propositions by using certain *parameters* (phrases like "things identical to," "persons identical to," and so on). Thus, "Socrates is a good philosopher" may be reexpressed as "All persons identical to Socrates are good philosophers." Another example: "This dogwood is now blossoming" may be reexpressed as "All things identical with this dogwood are things that are now blossoming."

4.   Statements containing spatial and temporal *adverbs,* such as "everywhere" or "sometimes," may be translated into categorical propositions by employing the words "places" and "times," respectively. Similarly, statements containing *pronouns* like "whoever" or "whatever" may be translated by employing the words "persons" and "things," respectively. For example, "Snow is everywhere" may be reexpressed as "All places are places in which there is snow." "John never goes to school" may be reexpressed as "No times are times when John goes to school."

5.   Many statements in ordinary language have implied but *unexpressed quantifiers.* These statements may be translated by making the quantifier explicit. Thus "Donkeys are stubborn" may be reexpressed as "All donkeys are stubborn things." "Children are present" may be reexpressed as "Some children are things that are present."

6.   Many statements in ordinary language have *nonstandard quantifiers* that are expressed by words other than the three allowable quantifiers of categorical propositions. In such cases, the statements may often be reexpressed in terms of the three allowable quantifiers. Thus "Several books on this shelf are difficult" may be reexpressed as "Some books on this shelf are books that are difficult to read." In this connection it should be noted that "All *S* are not *P*" is not standard form categorical proposition. It may be reexpressed, however, either as "No *S* are *P*" or as "Some *S* are not *P*," depending on its meaning. Thus "All that glitters is not gold" may be reexpressed as "Some things that glitter are not things made of gold."

7.   Certain *conditional statements* can be reexpressed as categorical propositions. For example, "If a man is tired, then he is hungry" can be reexpressed as "All tired men are hungry men." As in this example, the conditionals that can be translated have the same subject in both the antecedent and the consequent. They always translate as universal categorical propositions. Statements containing "unless" can also often be translated. Thus "Dogs are happy unless they are beaten" becomes "All unbeaten dogs are happy dogs."

8. *Exclusive propositions* (those that involve the words "only" and "none but") may also be translated. Thus "Only dogs are happy animals" becomes "All happy animals are dogs." "None but natural techniques are allowed" becomes "All techniques that are allowed are natural techniques."

9. Statements beginning with *"the only"* are different from those beginning with "only." Usually the words "the only" may simply be replaced with the word "all." Thus "The only flowers I like are roses" is translated as "All flowers that I like are roses."

10. *Exceptive propositions*, like "All except *S* are *P*," must be translated as pairs of conjoined categorical propositions, such as "No *S* are *P*, and all non-*S* are *P*." Exceptive propositions ("all except," "all but") should not be confused with exclusive propositions.

Sample Exercises from Exercise 4.7. Part I

1. Any bank that makes too many risky loans will fail.

   This may be reexpressed as:
   All banks that make too many risky loans are banks that will fail.

2. Women military officers are not eligible for combat duty.

   This may be reexpressed as:
   No women military officers are persons eligible for combat duty.

3. Terrorist attacks succeed whenever security measures are lax.

   This may be reexpressed as:
   All terrorist attacks are efforts that succeed whenever security measures are lax.

4. Bromine is extractable from sea water.

   This proposition is a difficult one to translate. Its translation depends crucially on the parameter that is used. If, for example, we were to use the parameter "substances," then the proposition could be translated as:

   All substances that are bromine are substances that are extractable from sea water.

   This translation, despite being an **A** proposition, would not imply that every bit or parcel of bromine is extractable from sea water. For instance, it does not imply that some bit of bromine on some distant star is extractable from sea water on earth. Because of considerations about such distant bits of bromine, we could not translate this sentence as:

   All parcels (or: bits) of matter composed of bromine are extractable from sea water.

   With a parameter like "bits of matter that are composed of bromine," therefore, we would have to translate this sentence as an **I** proposition:

   Some bits of matter composed of bromine are extractable from sea water.

   As this example shows, we must be very careful when translating propositions about substances.

Additional Exercises for Section 4.7

Reexpress the following statements as categorical propositions.

1. Only the strong survive.

2. No one not in the club may vote.

3. Wherever you go I will follow.

4. Any tiger is fierce.

5. The only men who will be promoted are sergeants.

6. Only sergeants are men who will be promoted.

7. Elephants are big.

8. All but miscreants will go unpunished.

9. George Washington was the first U.S. president.

10. My father was a carpenter.

11. Men at work. (as on a sign)

12. A whale is a mammal.

13. I will meet you anytime.

14. Dogs are not five-legged.

15. If a man is well-fed, he is content.

16. No one likes broccoli.

17. If you likes broccoli, you'll love spinach.

18. A city is prosperous if it has industry.

19. Several people did not like the movie.

20. When you first called, I was surprised.

5
CATEGORICAL
SYLLOGISMS

5.1 STANDARD MOOD, FORM, AND FIGURE

A *syllogism* is a two-premise deductive argument. More specifically, a *categorical syllogism* is an argument in which both the premises and the conclusion are categorical propositions. Furthermore, these three propositions contain a total of three different terms, each used exactly twice, and none is used twice in the same proposition of the argument. In the following discussion, "syllogism" means "categorical syllogism."

The predicate term of the conclusion is called the *major term* of the syllogism. It occurs in only one of the premises, and that premise is called the *major premise* of the syllogism. The subject term of the conclusion is called the *minor term* of the syllogism. It occurs in the premise that does not contain the major term, which is called the *minor premise* of the syllogism. The remaining, or third, term is called the *middle term* of the syllogism. It occurs once in the major premise and once in the minor premise.

A categorical syllogism is in *standard form* if the major premise is listed first, the minor premise second, and the conclusion third. The *mood* of a syllogism in standard form is a list of three letters, where each of these letters is **A**, **E**, **I**, or **O**. The first letter designates the categorical type of the major premise, the second letter the categorical type of the minor premise, and the third letter the categorical type of the conclusion.

The *figure* of a standard form categorical syllogism is a number from 1 to 4 that designates the *arrangement* of its three terms. Thus, Figure 1 designates the arrangement

$$...M...P$$
$$...S...M$$
$$...S...P$$

(Here "S" denotes the minor term, the subject of the conclusion; "P" denotes the term, the predicate of the conclusion; and "M" denotes the middle term.)

Figure 2 designates the arrangement

$$...P...M$$
$$...S...M$$
$$...S...P$$

Figure 3 designates the arrangement

$$...M...P$$
$$...M...S$$
$$...S...P$$

Figure 4 designates the arrangement

$$...P...M$$
$$\underline{...M...S}$$
$$...S...P$$

The mood and figure of a categorical syllogism can be determined by putting its major premise first, its minor premise second, and its conclusion third, and then noting both the types of its propositions and the arrangement of its terms.

Moreover, a mood and figure designation, such as **AII**-2, can be fleshed out by simply drawing the form of the indicated figure (in this case, Figure 2) and then writing in the quantifiers and copulas to make each of the propositions match the indicated mood (in this case, **AII**). Thus, **AII**-2 can be fleshed out as

All *P* are *M*.
Some *S* are *M*.
Some *S* are *P*.

Each such fleshed-out syllogism represents a logical form of an actual syllogism. Assuming that there are no semantic connections among the terms of the syllogism, a syllogism is valid if and only if its form is valid. In the modern interpretation of categorical propositions, exactly fifteen of the mood and figure designations represent valid forms:

Figure 1: **AAA, EAE, AII, EIO**
Figure 2: **EAE, AEE, EIO, AOO**
Figure 3: **IAI, AII, OAO, EIO**
Figure 4: **AEE, IAI, EIO**

In the traditional interpretation of categorical propositions, nine other mood and figure designations represent valid forms:

Figure 1: **AAI, EAO**
Figure 2: **AEO, EAO**
Figure 3: **AAI, EAO**
Figure 4: **AEO, EAO, AAI**

Sample Exercises from Exercise 5.1. Part I

1. All neutron stars are things that produce intense gravity.

   All neutron stars are extremely dense objects.

   Therefore, all extremely dense objects are things that produce intense gravity.

   P = things that produce intense gravity

   S = extremely dense objects

   M = neutron stars

   The mood and figure of this syllogism is **AAA**-3. It is invalid.

2. No insects that eat mosquitoes are insects that should be killed.

   All dragonflies are insects that eat mosquitoes.

   Therefore, no dragonflies are insects that should be killed.

$P =$ insects that should be killed

$S =$ dragonflies

$M =$ insects that eat mosquitoes

The mood and figure of this syllogism is **EAE**-1. It is unconditionally valid.

Sample Exercises from Exercise 5.1. Part II

1. No Republicans are Democrats, so no Republicans are big spenders, since all big spenders are Democrats.

   $P =$ big spenders (since this is the predicate of the conclusion, "no Republicans are big spenders")

   $S =$ Republicans (since this is the subject of the conclusion, "no Republicans are big spenders")

   $M =$ Democrats (since this term occurs in both premises)

   In standard form this argument is:

   All big spenders are Democrats.

   No Republicans are Democrats.

   Therefore, no Republicans are big spenders.

   The mood and figure of this syllogism is **AEE**-2. It is unconditionally valid.

2. Some latchkey children are not kids who can stay out of trouble, for some youngsters prone to boredom are latchkey children, and no kids who can stay out of trouble are youngsters prone to boredom.

   $P =$ kids who can stay out of trouble (since this is the predicate of the conclusion, "Some latchkey children are not kids who can stay out of trouble")

   $S =$ latchkey children (since this is the subject of the conclusion, "Some latchkey children are not kids who can stay out of trouble")

   $M =$ youngsters prone to boredom (since this term occurs in both premises)

   In standard form this argument is:

   No kids who can stay out of trouble are youngsters prone to boredom.

   Some youngsters prone to boredom are latchkey children.

   Therefore, some latchkey children are not kids who can stay out of trouble.

   The mood and figure of this syllogism is **EIO**-4. It is unconditionally valid.

Additional Exercises for Section 5.1

I. Flesh out the following mood and figure designations. Determine whether the resultant syllogism is valid (according to the modern interpretation of categorical propositions) by checking the mood and figure designation against the list of valid syllogisms.

1.	**AII**-2	6.	**EAE**-2
2.	**AAA**-3	7.	**AOI**-4
3.	**EIO**-4	8.	**EEO**-3
4.	**IEA**-1	9.	**EOO**-1
5.	**OOO**-2	10.	**EAE**-4

II. Identify the major term (*P*), the minor term (*S*), and the middle term (*M*) of the following syllogisms. Place them into standard form (if they are not already in standard form). Identify their mood and figure. By checking the list of valid syllogisms, determine whether they are valid or invalid (according to the modern interpretation of categorical propositions).

1. No men are islands.
    All islands are continents.
    Some continents are not men.

2. No islands are men.
    Some islands are continents.
    Some continents are not men.

3. Some seals are walruses.
    No walruses are tigers.
    Some tigers are not seals.

4. All elephants are pachyderms.
    Some pachyderms are not large animals.
    Some elephants are not large animals.

5. No dogs are cats.
    All cats are felines.
    No dogs are felines.

6. Some dogs are cockers.
    All cockers are spaniels.
    Some spaniels are not dogs.

7. Some horses are stallions, for some horses are roans, and all roans are stallions.

8. No ants are insects. So no grasshoppers are insects, since all ants are grasshoppers.

9. Since all figurines are art objects, some art objects are not paintings, for no paintings are figurines.

10. No drivers are racers, since all racers are speeders and no speeders are drivers.

60

5.2   VENN DIAGRAMS

Venn diagrams provide a convenient technique for testing the validity of categorical syllogisms. In using Venn diagrams in conjunction with categorical syllogisms, the general conventions specified in Section 4.3 prevail, except that we now have three terms and three circles.

To use a Venn diagram to test for the validity of a categorical syllogism, follow this procedure:

1.   Enter the information of the premises into the diagram. (Do not enter the conclusion.)
2.   Look at the resulting diagram to see whether it implies the information of the conclusion. If it does, the syllogism is valid. If it does not, the syllogism is invalid.

Several pointers will facilitate using this procedure:

1.   Diagram universal premises before particular premises.
2.   When diagramming a premise, concentrate only on the two circles representing the terms of that premise. The third circle can usually be ignored.
3.   When placing an "X" in the diagram, note that it always goes into an area that is split by the third (largely ignored) circle. This third circle divides that area into two parts. If neither of these parts has been shaded, the "X" is placed on the line from the third circle that divides the two parts. If one of these parts has been shaded, the "X" is placed in the unshaded part. (*Note*: In a diagram for a categorical syllogism, it will never happen that both parts are shaded.)

Sample Exercises from Exercise 5.2. Part I

1.   All corporations that overcharge their customers are unethical businesses.
     Some unethical businesses are investor-owned utilities.
     Therefore, some investor-owned utilities are corporations that overcharge their customers.

     The form of this argument is **AII**-4. Its Venn diagram is:

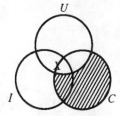

     It is invalid (both from a modern, Boolean standpoint and from the traditional viewpoint).

2.   No AIDS victims are persons who pose an immediate threat to the lives of others.
     Some kindergarten children are AIDS victims.
     Therefore, some kindergarten children are not persons who pose an immediate threat to the lives of others.

The form of this argument is **EIO**-1. Its Venn diagram is:

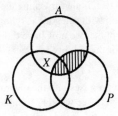

It is valid (both from a modern, Boolean standpoint and from the traditional viewpoint).

Sample Exercises from Exercise 5.2. Part II

1. No *P* are *M*.
   All *S* are *M*.

   The Venn diagram for these two premises is:

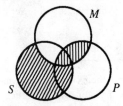

   From the diagram it may be seen that the conclusion "No *S* are *P*" may validly be drawn.

2. Some *P* are not *M*.
   Some *M* are *S*.

   The Venn diagram for these two premises is:

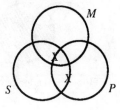

   From the diagram it may be seen that no conclusion may validly be drawn.

Additional Exercises for Section 5.2

Construct Venn diagrams for the twenty examples in "Additional Exercises for Section 5.1, Parts I and II" and use them to determine whether the syllogisms are valid or invalid. Check your answers against the list of valid syllogisms (according to the modern interpretation of the categorical propositions).

5.3   RULES AND FALLACIES

Valid syllogisms conform to certain rules, and these rules may accordingly be used as crosschecks to the Venn diagram test for validity. Following are five rules. When one of these rules is broken, a corresponding formal fallacy is committed. Moreover, if none of the rules is broken, then the syllogism is valid. The first two rules have to do with the distribution of terms, and the last three have to do with the quality and quantity of the propositions in the syllogisms.

In using Rules 1 and 2, recall that

In the **A** proposition, *S* is distributed, *P* is undistributed.
In the **E** proposition, *S* and *P* are both distributed.
In the **I** proposition, *S* and *P* are both undistributed.
In the **O** proposition, *S* is undistributed, *P* is distributed.

Rule 1: The middle term must be distributed in at least one of the premises.
Fallacy: If this rule is broken, the fallacy committed is *undistributed middle*.

Example: All *P* are *M*.
All *S* are *M*.
All *S* are *P*.   Here *M* is undistributed in both premises.

Rule 2: If a term is distributed in the conclusion, it must be distributed in the premise.

Fallacy: If this rule is broken, the fallacy committed is either *illicit major* (if *P* is distributed in the conclusion but undistributed in the major premise) or *illicit minor* (if *S* is distributed in the conclusion but undistributed in the minor premise).

Example: All *M* are *P*.
All *S* are *M*.
No *S* are *P*.   Here *P* is distributed in the conclusion but undistributed in the major premise. (illicit major)

Example: All *P* are *M*.
All *M* are *S*.
No *S* are *P*.   Here *S* is distributed in the conclusion but undistributed in the minor premise. (illicit minor)

Rule 3: Two negative premises are not allowed.

Fallacy: If this rule is broken, the fallacy committed is *exclusive premises*.

Example: No *P* are *M*.
No *S* are *M*.
No *S* are *P*.   Here both premises are negative.

Rule 4: A negative premise requires a negative conclusion, and a negative conclusion requires a negative premise.

Notice that, since by Rule 3, two negative premises are not allowed, Rule 4 means that a negative conclusion can occur only when there is *exactly one* negative premise.

<table>
<tr><td>Fallacy:</td><td>If this rule is broken, the fallacy committed is either drawing a negative conclusion from affirmative premises or drawing an affirmative conclusion from a negative premise.</td></tr>
</table>

Example: All *P* are *M*.
  All *S* are *M*.
  No *S* are *P*.   Here a negative conclusion is drawn from affirmative premises.

Example: No *P* are *M*.
  Some *S* are *M*.
  Some *S* are *P*.   Here an affirmative conclusion is drawn from a negative premise.

Rule 5: If both premises are universal, the conclusion cannot be particular.

Fallacy: If this rule is broken, the *existential fallacy* is committed.

Example: All *P* are *M*.
  All *S* are *M*.
  Some *S* are *P*.

Note: Rule 5 applies only to the modern interpretation of the categorical propositions. On the traditional interpretation of the categorical propositions there is no existential fallacy. Thus, a syllogism that breaks *only* Rule 5 will be valid from the traditional (Aristotelian) standpoint, though not from the modern (Boolean) standpoint.

Sample Exercises from Exercise 5.3

1. **AAA**-3

Fleshed out, this becomes:

  All *M* are *P*.
  All *M*   *S*.
  All *S* are *P*.

Since *S* is distributed in the conclusion but not in the minor premise, this syllogism commits the fallacy of illicit minor.

The Venn diagram for this argument is:

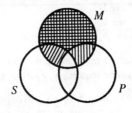

2. **IAI**-2

   Fleshed out, this becomes:

   > Some *P* are *M*.
   > All *S* are *M*.
   > Some *S* are *P*.

   Since *M* is undistributed in both premises, this syllogism commits the fallacy of undistributed middle.

   The Venn diagram for this argument is:

   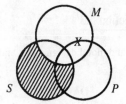

3. **EIO**-1

   Fleshed out, this becomes:

   > No *M* are *P*.
   > Some *S* are *M*.
   > Some *S* are not *P*.

   This syllogism commits none of the fallacies and is accordingly valid.

   The Venn diagram for this argument is:

   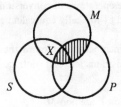

4. **AAI**-2

   Fleshed out, this becomes:

   > All *P* are *M*.
   > All *S* are *M*.
   > Some *S* are *P*.

   Since a particular conclusion is drawn from two universal premises, this syllogism commits the existential fallacy. Since *M* is undistributed in both premises, it also commits the fallacy of undistributed middle.

The Venn diagram for this argument is:

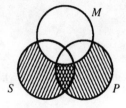

Additional Exercises for Section 5.3

Flesh out the following figure and mood designations and test the result for validity using the five rules.

1. **AAA**-4		6. **OAO**-4
2. **AAA**-1		7. **IEA**-1
3. **EII**-2		8. **AEA**-3
4. **EEE**-3		9. **AEE**-1
5. **AII**-3		10. **IAI**-3

5.4   REDUCING THE NUMBER OF TERMS

Many two-premise arguments contain negated terms, so that the number of terms in the entire argument exceeds three. Thus, these arguments are not categorical syllogisms in the strict sense. Nevertheless, through use of the operations of conversion, obversion, and contraposition, such arguments can often be replaced by logically equivalent arguments that *are* categorical syllogisms in the strict sense.

The important things to remember in employing these operations are that conversion may be applied only to **E** and **I** propositions and that contraposition may be applied only to **A** and **O** propositions.

> Example: All non-*P* are non-*M*.
> All non-*M* are non-*S*.
> No *S* are non-*P*.

Applying contraposition to both premises and obversion to the conclusion, we may replace this argument with the logically equivalent argument

> All *M* are *P*.
> All *S* are *M*.
> All *S* are *P*.

This syllogism is, of course, of the form **AAA**-1 and is valid. Consequently, the original argument is valid.

Sample Exercise from Exercise 5.4

1. Some intelligible statements are true statements, because all unintelligible statements are meaningless statements and some false statements are meaningful statements.

> Let I = intelligible statements, T = true statements, and M = meaningful statements. Then, ordering premises and conclusion, the argument becomes:

> > Some non-T are M.
> > All non-I are non-M.
> > Some I are T.

> By applying conversion and then obversion to the first premise, and contraposition to the second premise, we obtain:

> > Some M are not T.
> > All M are I.
> > Some I are T.

This is the syllogism **OAI**-3. It commits the fallacy of drawing an affirmative conclusion from a negative premise.

Additional Exercises for Section 5.4

By rearranging propositions and applying the operations of conversion; obversion, and contraposition, make these arguments into standard form categorical syllogisms. Identify whether they are valid or invalid.

1. No one is crazy and some financiers are not non-persons. So some financiers are sane.

2. All valid arguments are intelligible ones. So some chains of reasoning are not valid arguments, since some chains of reasoning are intelligible arguments.

3. Some happy persons are not solvents, since some bankers are insolvent and no bankers are happy persons.

4. All snacks are fattening foods and all fattening foods are non-nutritious. So all nutritious foods are non-snacks.

5. Some scholars are not felons. The reason for this is that no felons are innocent and some scholars are not guilty.

5.5   ORDINARY LANGUAGE ARGUMENTS

Many two-premise arguments in ordinary language do not look much like standard form categorical syllogisms. However, by a judicious process of translation, some of them may be converted into standard form categorical syllogisms and then tested for validity using the techniques presented in this chapter. Perhaps the best way to see this is to consider the solved exercises from the text.

Sample Exercises from Exercise 5.5

1. Inside traders are the only people who make lots of money on the stock market, and Ivan Boesky made millions. Thus, Ivan Boesky was an inside trader.

   In order to translate this argument into a standard-form categorical syllogism, we must first agree to regard "making millions" and "making lots of money" as synonymous. If we do not do this, we would have an "enthymematic" argument which would turn out to be a "sorites" when fully expressed. (See the following two sections for the meaning of "enthymeme" and "sorites.")

   This argument may be reexpressed as:

   > All persons who make lots of money on the stock market are inside traders.
   > All persons identical to Ivan Boesky are persons who make lots of money on the stock market.
   > Therefore, all persons identical to Ivan Boesky are inside traders.

   This is the syllogism **AAA**-1 and is valid.

2. Whenever suicide rates decline we can infer that people's lives are better adjusted. Accordingly, since suicide rates have been declining in recent years, we can infer that people's lives have been better adjusted in recent years.

   This argument may be reexpressed as:

   > All times in which suicide rates are declining are times in which (we can infer that) people's lives are better adjusted.
   > All times in recent years are times in which suicide rates are declining.
   > Therefore, all times in recent years are times in which (we can infer that) people's lives are better adjusted.

   This is the syllogism **AAA**-1 and is valid.

Additional Exercises for Section 5.5

Reexpress the following arguments as standard form categorical syllogisms, and test them for validity using the five rules for valid syllogisms.

1. I like all drinks and this is a drink, so I like it.

2. If you go to town, you buy a dress. Since you went to town today, you must have bought a dress today.

3. Nothing immoral is fattening, and overeating is fattening. It follows that overeating is not immoral.

4. Wherever you go I will follow, but I won't follow you to Bali. So you won't go to Bali.

5. If you have any money, we will spend it. Some of your money is ill-gotten gains. So we will spend some ill-gotten gains.

5.6 ENTHYMEMES

An enthymeme is an argument that is expressible as a categorical syllogism but that is missing either a premise or the conclusion. To evaluate an enthymeme, supply the missing premise or conclusion, express the syllogism in standard form, and apply the usual tests for validity.

Sample Exercises from Exercise 5.6. Part I

1. Some police chiefs undermine the evenhanded enforcement of the law, because anyone who fixes parking tickets does that.

    This enthymeme is missing the premise: Some police chiefs are persons who fix parking tickets.

    Thus, the filled-out valid syllogism, in standard form, is:

    > All persons who fix parking tickets are persons who undermine the evenhanded enforcement of the law.
    > Some police chiefs are persons who fix parking tickets.
    > Therefore, some police chiefs are persons who undermine the evenhanded enforcement of the law.

    This syllogism has the form **AII**-1.

2. Any drastic decline in animal life is a cause for alarm, and the current decline in frogs and toads is drastic.

    This enthymeme is missing the conclusion: The current decline in frogs and toads is a cause for alarm.

    Thus, the filled-out valid syllogism, in standard form, is:

    > All drastic declines in animal life are causes for alarm.
    > All current declines in frogs and toads are drastic declines in animal life.
    > Therefore, all current declines in frogs and toads are causes for alarm.

    This syllogism has the form **AAA**-1.

5.7 SORITES

A *sorites* is a sequence of categorical syllogisms in which the intermediate conclusions have been omitted. A sorites is in *standard form* when each of the component propositions is a standard form categorical proposition, when the predicate term of the conclusion is in the first premise, when each term occurs exactly twice, and when each premise after the first has a term in common with the preceding one. To evaluate a sorites, express it in standard form, supply the intermediate conclusions, and then break the sorites up into its separate component categorical syllogisms; then test each of the syllogisms for validity. The sorites is valid if each component is valid. Otherwise, it is invalid.

1. No *B* are *C*.
    Some *D* are *C*.
    All *A* are *B*.
    Some *D* are not *A*.

    In standard form this sorites becomes:

    > All *A* are *B*.
    > No *B* are *C*.
    > Some *D* are *C*.
    > Some *D* are not *A*.

    The intermediate conclusion (supposed to follow from the first two premises) is: No *A* are *C*.

    Thus, the sorites breaks up into two syllogisms:

All *A* are *B*.		No *A* are *C*.
No *B* are *C*.	and	Some *D* are *C*.
No *A* are *C*.		Some *D* are not *A*.

    The Venn diagrams for these two syllogisms are:

    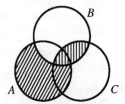 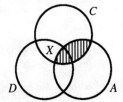

    Both are valid. Consequently, the sorites itself is valid.

2. No *C* are *D*.
    All *A* are *B*.
    Some *C* are not *B*.
    Some *D* are not *A*.

    In standard form this sorites becomes:

    > All *A* are *B*.
    > Some *C* are not *B*.
    > Some *C* are *D*.
    > Some *D* are not *A*.

    The intermediate conclusion is: Some *C* are not *A*.

    Thus, the sorites breaks up into two syllogisms:

All *A* are *B*.		Some *C* are not *A*.
Some *C* are not *B*.	and	No *C* are *D*.
Some *C* are not *A*.		Some *D* are not *A*.

The Venn diagrams for these two syllogisms are:

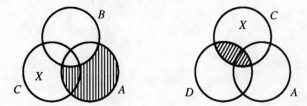

The first of these is valid, but the second is invalid. Thus, the sorites as a whole is invalid.

6

PROPOSITIONAL LOGIC

6.1 SYMBOLS AND TRANSLATION

As we have seen, a great deal of logic involves the search for valid argument forms. In *propositional logic* this quest continues. Here, however, the forms we are concerned with have as their fundamental elements symbols denoting entire statements or propositions. We may define a *simple (atomic)* statement as one containing no other statement as a component, and a *compound (molecular)* statement is one that contains at least one simple statement as a component. Upper case letters are used to denote atomic statements.

Propositional logic also relies on special symbols denoting *operators,* also called *connectives*—that is, words or groups of words that have the function of combining one or two propositions into a single larger proposition:

Connective	Name	Meaning
~	negation	not; it is not the case that
·	conjunction	and
∨	disjunction	or
⊃	conditional	if . . . then; only if
≡	biconditional	if and only if

Note: The conjunction sign also stands for words like "but," "however," "and also," and so forth. The disjunction sign stands for the *inclusive* "or," sometimes written as "and/or." The conditional sign is also used for phrases like "given that," "on the condition that," and so forth. The meaning of the biconditional is that the propositions flanking it are the same in truth value—that is, both true or both false. (See the text for further explanations of the meanings of the five basic connectives.)

If we let *A* and *B* be two propositions, the various relationships between *A* and *B* may be symbolized, using the five basic connectives. Some of the most important symbolizations are:

Combination	Translation
A is true.	*A*
A is false.	~*A*
A isn't so.	~*A*
Either *A* or *B* (or both).	*A* ∨ *B*
A unless *B*.	*A* ∨ *B**
A or else *B*.	*A* ∨ *B*
If *A*, then *B*.	*A* ⊃ *B*
A if *B*.	*B* ⊃ *A*

---

*A unless *B* may also be used in an "exclusive" sense, to be translated as "*A* ≡ ~*B*."

73

Combination	Translation
A only if B.	$A \supset B$
Only if A, B.	$B \supset A$
A if and only if B.	$A \equiv B$
A is a necessary condition for B.	$B \supset A$
A is a sufficient condition for B.	$A \supset B$
A necessary condition for A is B.	$A \supset B$
A sufficient condition of A is B.	$B \supset A$
A necessary and sufficient condition for A is B.	$A \equiv B$
A is a necessary and sufficient condition for B.	$A \equiv B$
Neither A nor B.	$\sim(A \lor B)$
Either not A or not B.	$\sim A \lor \sim B$
Neither not A nor not B.	$\sim(\sim A \lor \sim B)$
Both not A and not B.	$\sim A \cdot \sim B$
Not both A and B.	$\sim(A \cdot B)$

The connectives allow us to combine not only atomic propositions with one another but also an atomic proposition with a molecular one and molecular propositions with each other. When combining molecular propositions into larger molecular propositions, care must be taken to insert parentheses so that the combination is unambiguous. For example, the proposition $A \supset B \supset C$ is ambiguous: it may mean either $A \supset (B \supset C)$ or $(A \supset B) \supset C$, and these two propositions are not logically equivalent.

Sample Exercises from Exercise 6.1. Part I

1. New Zealand does not have nuclear weapons.
   Translation: ~N

2. Turkey is a member of NATO but Iraq is not.
   Translation: T · ~I

3. Either Brazil or Argentina destroys its rain forests.
   Translation: B ∨ A

4. Both Poland and Ireland outlaw abortion.
   Translation: P · I

Additional Exercises for Section 6.1

Translate the following into symbolizations of propositional logic, using the upper case letters A = Al goes to town, B = Betty goes to town, C = Cathy goes to town.

1. A1 and Betty do not both go to town.

2. Al and Betty both do not go to town.

3. Either Al or Cathy does not go to town, but Betty does go.

4. Neither Al nor Betty goes to town.

5. If Al or Betty goes to town, Cathy does not go.

74

6. Al goes to town only if Betty goes but Cathy doesn't

7. Al does not go to town if and only if both Betty and Cathy do.

8. A necessary condition of Al's not going to town is Betty's and Cathy's both not going.

9. A necessary and sufficient condition for Al's going to town is Betty's and Cathy's not both going.

10. If Al goes to town, then Betty goes to town if Cathy doesn't.

6.2   TRUTH FUNCTIONS

If the truth value of a molecular proposition is entirely determined by the truth values of its atomic components (independent of the specific meaning of these atomic components), then the molecular proposition is said to be a *truth function* of its components. All molecular propositions built up out of atomic propositions by means of the five connectives so far introduced are truth functions of the atomic propositions. Another way of expressing this fact is to say that the five connectives are themselves *truth functional connectives*.

We can express the truth functionality of the five connectives by showing in a list or table exactly how the connectives render the truth value of a molecular proposition computable from the truth values of its components. In order to do so, we need to introduce the idea of a *statement variable*: a variable that can represent any statement or proposition. Statement variables are represented by lower case letters, such as "p" and "q." When statement variables are combined by means of connectives, we have statement forms. For example, "p," "$p \vee q$," and "$p \cdot q$" are statement forms. When we substitute any propositions uniformly for the statement variables in a statement form, a statement is produced. Such a statement is called a *substitution instance* of the statement form.

With the notions of statement variable and statement form, we can now express the truth functionality of the connectives. For instance, consider negation. We may express its truth functionality thusly.

p	$\sim p$
T	F
F	T

This table means that, regardless of what proposition is used to replace "p," if it is true, then its negation is false (regardless of its meaning), and if it is false, then its negation is true (again regardless of its meaning).

The table for conjunction is as follows:

p	q	$p \cdot q$
T	T	T
T	F	F
F	T	F
F	F	F

The meaning of this table is that a conjunction of any two propositions is true when and only when both the left-hand conjunct and the right-hand conjunct are true (regardless of the meanings of these conjuncts).

The tables for other connectives are:

p	q	p ∨ q
T	T	T
T	F	T
F	T	T
F	F	F

p	q	p ⊃ q
T	T	T
T	F	F
F	T	T
F	F	T

p	q	p ≡ q
T	T	T
T	F	F
F	T	F
F	F	T

These tables are in effect rules for calculating the truth value of any molecular proposition built up from atomic propositions by means of the five connectives, provided that we are given truth values for the atomic propositions themselves. For instance, suppose A is the proposition "2 and 2 make 4," B is the proposition "Clinton is President (in 1993)," and C is the proposition "Austin is the capitol of California." Then the truth value of (A ∨ B) ⊃ C; that is, of "If either 2 and 2 make 4 or Clinton is president (in 1993), then Austin is the capital of California" can be computed to be false. For A ∨ B can be computed to be true from the table for disjunction (first row, where the left-hand disjunct and the right-hand disjunct are both true), and then the entire proposition's truth value can be computed from the table for the conditional (second row, where the left-hand member, the antecedent, is true and the right-hand member, the consequent, is false). The calculation may also be expressed as follows:

(A ∨ B) ⊃ C

In performing such calculations, the important thing to remember is to work from inside out, from simpler to more complex.

Sample Exercises from Exercise 6.2. Part II

1. It is not the case that Hitler ran the Third Reich.

    This is the form ~H. Since it is true that Hitler ran the Third Reich, the resulting proposition is false.

2. Nixon resigned the Presidency and Lincoln wrote the Gettysburg Address.

    This has the form N · L. Since it is true that Nixon resigned the Presidency and true that Lincoln wrote the Gettysburg Address, the resulting proposition is true.

3. Caesar conquered China, or Lindbergh crossed the Atlantic.

    This has the form C ∨ L. Since it is false that Caesar conquered China and true that Lindbergh crossed the Atlantic, the resulting proposition is true.

4. Hitler ran the Third Reich and Nixon did not resign the Presidency.

    This is the form H · ~N. Since it is true that Hitler ran the Third Reich, and false that Nixon did not resign the Presidency, the resulting proposition is false.

Additional Exercises for Section 6.2

Compute the truth values of the following propositions. Assume that *A*, *B*, and *C* are true propositions and that *X*, *Y*, and *Z* are propositions.

1. $A \supset (B \supset X)$
2. $\sim A \vee [X \supset (\sim X)]$
3. $(A \equiv X) \equiv (B \equiv Y)$
4. $(A \equiv Z) \equiv (X \equiv Y)$
5. $X \supset \sim(X \supset \sim X)$

6. $(A \vee X) \supset (Y \vee Z)$
7. $[(A \cdot B) \cdot C] \equiv [A \cdot (X \vee Y)]$
8. $[(\sim A) \equiv (\sim X)] \vee (Y \vee C)$
9. $[(X \supset Y) \supset \sim Y] \supset (\sim X)$
10. $[X \supset (\sim X \supset Y)] \supset [(Y \supset \sim Z) \supset X]$

6.3 TRUTH TABLES FOR PROPOSITIONS

In the previous section it was shown how a truth value could be calculated for any molecular proposition built up from the five connectives, given a particular set of truth values for its atomic constituents. Obviously, a truth value could be calculated for such a molecular proposition given *any* truth value assignment for its atomic constituents. The notion of a truth table for a proposition is the notion of a table in which, for *every* truth value assignment to the atomic constituents of a proposition, a truth value is calculated and expressed. For any *n* letters, there are 2^n possible truth assignments to these letters taken together. Thus, the truth table for a proposition composed of *n* atomic constituents will have 2^n rows in it, one row for each truth assignment.

For example, here is the truth table for $P \vee \sim Q$:

P	∨	~	Q
T	T	F	T
T	T	T	F
F	F	F	T
F	T	T	F

In the column representing the proposition as a whole, we may find all true's, or we may find all false's, or we may find a mixture (at least one true and at least one false). In the first event, the proposition is called a *logical truth* or a *tautology;* in the second case, it is called a *logical falsehood* or a *self-contradiction;* and in the third case, it is called a *contingency.*

Two propositions having the same letters as constituents are said to be *logically equivalent* if they have exactly the same columns in their truth tables. A little reflection will show that two propositions are logically equivalent if and only if the proposition obtained by combining them with the material equivalence sign ($\equiv$) is itself a tautology. Two propositions are logically *contradictory* if their columns are exactly the opposite (a T for every F and vice versa). A little reflection will show that two propositions are logically contradictory only when the proposition obtained by combining them with the material equivalence sign is a self-contradiction.

Two or more propositions are said to be mutually *consistent* if a truth table containing all the propositions has at least one line in which all the propositions have the truth value T. Equivalently: two or more propositions are *consistent* if the truth table for their conjunction has at least one line in which the conjunction has the truth value T. Similarly, two or more propositions are said to be mutually *inconsistent* if a truth table containing all the propositions does not have at least one line in which all the propositions have the truth value T.

Equivalently: two or more propositions are *inconsistent* if the truth table for their conjunction does not have at least one line in which the conjunction has the truth value T.

Sample Exercises from Exercise 6.3. Part I

1. N ⊃ (N ⊃ N)

```
T  T  T T T
F  T  F T F
```

The proposition is tautologous.

2. (G ⊃ G) ⊃ G

```
T T T  T  T
F T F  F  F
```

The proposition is contingent.

Sample Exercises from Exercise 6.3. Part II

1.

```
~D ∨ B        ~(D  ·  ~B)
F T  T  T      T  T F F T
F T  F  F      F  T T T F
T F  T  T      T  F F F T
T F  T  F      T  F F T F
```

The propositions are logically equivalent. They are also mutually consistent.

2.

```
F ·  M        ~(F ∨ M)
T  T  T       F  T T T
T  F  F       F  T T F
F  F  T       F  F T T
F  F  F       T  F F F
```

The propositions are neither logically equivalent nor logically contradictory. Moreover, they are mutually inconsistent.

3.

```
~K ⊃ L         K ⊃ ~L
F T  T  T       T  F F T
F T  T  F       T  T T F
T F  T  T       F  T F T
T F  F  F       F  T T F
```

The propositions are neither logically equivalent nor logically contradictory. They are, however, mutually consistent.

Additional Exercises for Section 6.3

I. By constructing truth tables, determine whether the following propositions are contradictions, tautologies, or contingencies.

1. $P \vee \sim P$		6. $(P \cdot Q) \supset P$	
2. $P \supset \sim P$		7. $P \supset (Q \supset P)$	
3. $P \cdot \sim P$		8. $[(P \vee Q) \cdot \sim P] \cdot \sim Q$	
4. $P \vee Q$		9. $[P \cdot (Q \supset P)] \equiv [Q \cdot (Q \supset P)]$	
5. $(P \vee Q) \supset P$		10. $[P \equiv (Q \equiv P)] \equiv [Q \equiv (P \equiv Q)]$	

II. By constructing truth tables, determine which of the following pairs are logically equivalent propositions. Determine also whether the propositions of each pair are mutually consistent.

1. P		$P \supset \sim P$
2. P		$\sim P \supset P$
3. $P \vee Q$		$\sim P \vee \sim Q$
4. $P \supset Q$		$\sim P \vee Q$
5. $P \equiv (Q \equiv P)$		Q

6.4   TRUTH TABLES FOR ARGUMENTS

Just as truth tables may be constructed for single propositions, so, too, may truth tables be constructed for arguments (which are, after all, collections of propositions). To do so, we must represent all the propositions of the argument in a single table. That is, a column must be made for each proposition in the argument. If the argument is in English, it must be symbolized first, letting capital letters stand for each atomic proposition in the argument. For example, the argument "If John is happy, then Sam is happy; John is happy; therefore, Sam is happy" may be represented by:

$J \supset S$
J
____
S

Its truth table may be represented by:

J	$\supset$	S	/	J	//	S
T	T	T		T		T
T	F	F		T		F
F	T	T		F		T
F	T	F		F		F

A truth table may be used to test an argument for validity in the following way. If there is a row in the table in which every premise is true and the conclusion is false, the argument is invalid. If there is no such row, the argument is valid. For example, the truth table above shows that the argument is valid—there is no row in which all the premises are true and the conclusion is false.

Notice that any argument with a tautological conclusion is valid and that any argument with mutually inconsistent premises (premises such that there is no row in the truth table in which all of them are true) is also valid.

Sample Exercises from Exercise 6.4. Part I

1. If national elections deteriorate into TV popularity contests, then smooth-talking morons will get elected. Therefore, if national elections do not deteriorate into popularity contests, then smooth-talking morons will not get elected.

   Translation: $N \supset S$ // $\sim N \supset \sim S$

T	T	T	F T T	T	F T
T	F	F	F T T	T	T F
F	T	T	T F F	F	F T
F	T	F	T F T	T	T F

   In the third row, the premise is true and the conclusion is false. So the argument is invalid.

2. Brazil has a huge foreign debt. Therefore, either Brazil or Argentina has a huge foreign debt.

   Translation: B // $B \lor A$

T	T	T	T
T	T	T	F
F	F	T	T
F	F	F	F

   There is no row in which the premise is true and the conclusion is false. So the argument is valid.

Additional Exercises for Section 6.4

Test the following symbolized arguments for validity using truth tables.

1. $P \lor Q / P \supset \sim P$ // Q
2. $P \supset Q / \sim P \supset P$ // Q
3. $P \lor Q$ // $P \cdot Q$
4. $P \cdot Q$ // $P \equiv Q$
5. $P \cdot \sim Q$ // $P \equiv Q$
6. $P \supset Q / Q \supset R$ // $R \supset P$
7. $\sim(P \equiv Q) / \sim Q$ // P
8. $\sim P \lor Q / \sim Q \lor R$ // $Q \equiv P$
9. P / Q // $R \lor \sim R$
10. $P \lor Q / P \supset \sim P / \sim Q$ // R

6.5   INDIRECT TRUTH TABLES

The indirect truth table technique—also known as the shorter truth table technique—for testing for the validity of arguments is usually a faster method of testing for validity than constructing an entire truth table. It is based on the fact that an argument is invalid if and only if there is at least one row in its truth table in which all the premises are true and the conclusion false. Instead of constructing the entire table, we may attempt to construct a row in which the premises are true and the conclusion false. If we succeed in doing so, the argument is invalid. If we are unsuccessful—if the assumption that there is a row in which all premises are true and the conclusion is false leads to a contradictory truth assignment to one or more letters—then the argument is valid.

To apply the indirect technique, we must try to find a truth assignment to the letters of an argument which makes the premises true and the conclusion false. If our attempt is successful, the argument is shown to be invalid. If our attempt leads to a contradictory assignment to one or more letters, the argument is valid.

Example: Consider the valid argument $P \supset Q$ / P // Q. This is an instance of *modus ponens* and is valid. If we try to make premises true and conclusion false, we must at least make Q (the conclusion) false and P (the second premise) true. But with P true and Q false, the first premise, $P \supset Q$, cannot be made true. This method shows the argument to be valid.

Example: Consider the invalid argument $P \supset Q$ / Q // P. Here we must make P (the conclusion) false and Q (the second premise) true. Now $P \supset Q$ becomes true and we have invented a truth assignment that makes all the premises true and the conclusion false. This method shows the argument to be invalid.

The indirect (or: shorter) truth table technique may also be used to ascertain whether the propositions in a given set are mutually consistent. To apply the technique for this purpose, we attempt to construct a row of a truth table in which all the propositions of the given set are true. If we succeed in doing so, then the propositions in the set are consistent. If, however, the assumption that there is such a row leads inevitably to a contradictory truth assignment to one or more letters, then the set of propositions is inconsistent.

Sample Exercises from Exercise 6.5

1. $B \supset C$
    $\underline{\sim C}$
    $\sim B$

    In order that the second premise should be true, C must be false. In order that the conclusion should be false, B must be true. But if B is true and C is false, then the first premise must be false. Thus, there is no way to make all the premises true and the conclusion false. Hence, the argument is valid.

2. $\sim E \vee F$
    $\underline{\sim E}$
    $\sim F$

    The only way to make the conclusion false is to make F true. The only way to make the second premise true is to make E false. With F true and E false, the first premise becomes true, so we have an assignment making premises true and conclusion false. Thus, the argument is invalid.

3. $P \supset (Q \cdot R)$
   $\underline{R \supset S}$
   $P \supset S$

In order that the conclusion should be false, P must be true and S must be false. Given that S is false, the only way for the second premise to be true is that R be false. But if P is true, S is false, and R is false, then—since R is false—it must be the case that $Q \cdot R$ is false, regardless of what truth value Q has. It follows that $P \supset (Q \cdot R)$ must be false, and, thus, that there is no way to make all the premises true and the conclusion false. Hence, the argument is valid.

4. $\underline{\sim(I \equiv J)}$
   $\sim(I \supset J)$

This example is a little more complex than the two preceding ones. There are *two* ways to make the premise true, namely with I true and J false or with I false and J true. If I is true and J is false, then the conclusion is true, so this assignment does not lead to a demonstration that the argument is invalid. But with I false and J true, the conclusion becomes false. This, therefore, is an assignment making the premise true and the conclusion false; it accordingly shows the argument to be invalid.

Additional Exercises for Section 6.5

Determine whether the following arguments are valid or invalid, using the indirect truth table technique.

1. $P \supset Q$
   $\underline{P \cdot R}$
   $Q \cdot R$

2. $P \vee Q$
   $\overline{\sim Q \supset P}$

3. $P \supset Q$
   $\overline{P \supset (P \cdot Q)}$

4. $P \supset \sim P$
   $\underline{P \vee Q}$
   Q

5. $P \supset Q$
   $\underline{\sim Q \supset Q}$
   $\sim P \supset P$

6. $P \supset Q$
   $\underline{Q \supset \sim Q}$
   $P \supset \sim P$

7. $P \equiv Q$
   $\underline{Q}$
   P

8. P
   $\underline{Q}$
   $P \equiv Q$

9. P
   $\underline{\sim Q}$
   $P \equiv Q$

10. $P \vee Q$
    $\overline{P \equiv Q}$

6.6   ARGUMENT FORMS AND FALLACIES

Many arguments in propositional logic are substitution instances of argument forms that have specific names and are valid (in the sense that any substitution instance of them is valid). Six such valid forms will be discussed in this section. Some arguments in propositional logic have invalid forms with specific names. With an invalid form, substitution instances are not, in general, valid arguments. Several such invalid forms will be discussed here.

Valid Forms

Disjunctive syllogism (DS)

$$p \lor q$$
$$\underline{\sim p}$$
$$q$$

Hypothetical syllogism (HS)

$$p \supset q$$
$$\underline{q \supset r}$$
$$p \supset r$$

Modus ponens (MP)

$$p \supset q$$
$$\underline{p}$$
$$q$$

Modus tollens (MT)

$$p \supset q$$
$$\underline{\sim q}$$
$$\sim p$$

Constructive dilemma (CD)

$$(p \supset q) \cdot (r \supset s)$$
$$\underline{p \lor r}$$
$$q \lor s$$

Destructive dilemma (DD)

$$(p \supset q) \cdot (r \supset s)$$
$$\underline{\sim q \lor \sim s}$$
$$\sim p \lor \sim r$$

Invalid Forms

Fallacy of affirming the consequent (AC)

$$p \supset q$$
$$\underline{q}$$
$$p$$

Fallacy of denying the antecedent (DA)

$$p \supset q$$
$$\underline{\sim p}$$
$$\sim q$$

Notice that the invalid form affirming the consequent is easily confused with *modus ponens*. Similarly, the invalid form denying the antecedent is easily confused with *modus tollens*. Another invalid form, nameless but easily confused with the disjunctive syllogism, is:

$$p \lor q$$
$$\underline{p}$$
$$q$$

Sample Exercises from Exercise 6.6. Part I

1. $N \supset C$
   $\underline{\sim C}$
   $\sim N$

   This argument is *modus tollens*.

2. $S \supset F$
   $\underline{F \supset \sim L}$
   $S \supset \sim L$

   This argument is hypothetical syllogism.

3. $A \lor {\sim}Z$

    $\underline{{\sim}Z}$

    A

    This is an invalid argument form.

4. $(S \supset {\sim}P) \cdot ({\sim}S \supset D)$

    $\underline{S \lor {\sim}S}$

    ${\sim}P \lor D$

    This argument is constructive dilemma.

Additional Exercises for Section 6.6

Identify the forms of the following valid arguments.

1. If Al goes to town, then so will Betty. Al goes to town. So then, will Betty.

2. If Al goes to town, then so will Betty. Betty will not go to town. So, Al does not go to town.

3. Either Al goes to town or Betty stays home. Al does not go to town. So Betty stays home.

4. If Al goes to town, then Betty stays home. But if Betty stays home, then supper will not be purchased. So if Al goes to town, supper will not be purchased.

5. If Al goes to town, then Betty stays home. But if Al does not go to town, then Cathy stays home. Since Al either goes or doesn't go to town, either Betty stays home or Cathy stays home.

6. If Al plays in the tournament, then Betty will win it, and if Kenny plays in the tournament, then Cathy will win it. Either Betty will not win the tournament or Cathy will not win it. So either Al will not play in it or Kenny will not play in it.

7. If no one likes fish in this town, then this store will soon be bankrupt. But no one does like fish in this town. The conclusion is inevitable that this store will soon be bankrupt.

8. If John came home last night on time, his mother is happy today. His mother is not happy today. Therefore, John did not come home last night on time.

9. Either you go to class or I go to class. But you don't go. So I go.

10. If I represent myself in court, then I have a fool for a lawyer. But if I have a fool for a lawyer, then I have a fool for a client. So if I represent myself in court then I have a fool for a client.

7
NATURAL DEDUCTION IN PROPOSITIONAL LOGIC

7.1   RULES OF IMPLICATION I

Every substitution instance of a valid argument form is valid. This fact is the key to understanding *natural deduction,* a method of demonstrating the validity of arguments in propositional logic. In natural deduction, certain valid argument forms (and eventually certain forms of logical equivalences) are used as *rules* for deducing a proposition from one or more others. For example, since $p \supset q / p // q$ is a valid argument form, then from, say $A \supset B$ and A, B can be validly deduced. A *proof* or *derivation* of an argument is a sequence of propositions that leads from the premises of the argument to its conclusion in the following way: each proposition in the sequence is either itself one of the premises of the argument or else can be deduced from one or more *previous* members of the sequence by means of one of the rules of deduction.

It can be shown in detail—and it is more or less intuitively clear—that any argument for which a proof exists is a valid argument.

As a matter of fact, any valid argument form (or any form of logical equivalence) can be used as a rule of deduction. For the purpose of simplicity, most systems of natural deduction employ only a small number of forms as *rules of inference.* In this test there are eighteen such rules. The first four are

1. $p \supset q$ *modus ponens* (MP)
     $\underline{p\qquad}$
     q

2. $p \supset q$ *modus tollens* (MT)
     $\underline{\sim q}$
     $\sim p$

3. $p \supset q$ hypothetical syllogism (HS)
     $\underline{q \supset r}$
     $p \supset r$

4. $p \vee q$ disjunctive syllogism (DS)
     $\underline{\sim p}$
     q

The basic task in mastering natural deduction is to learn to construct proofs. This task is not always simple and straightforward. The text gives a number of rules of thumb for constructing derivations, but there is no substitute for practice. In some ways natural deduction is like the game of chess; in order to play it well, one must first learn the permitted moves by heart and then, with practice, acquire a "feel" for the strategy of the activity.

Sample Exercises from Exercise 7.1. Part II

(1) 1. $(G \equiv J) \vee (B \supset P)$
    2. $\sim(G \equiv J)$ / $B \equiv P$
    3. $B \equiv P$ 1, 2, DS

(2) 1. $(K \cdot O) \supset (N \vee T)$
    2. $K \cdot O$ / $N \vee T$
    3. $N \vee T$ 1, 2, MP

(3) 1. $(M \vee P) \supset \sim K$
    2. $D \supset (M \vee P)$ / $D \supset \sim K$
    3. $D \supset \sim K$ 1, 2, HS

(4) 1. $\sim\sim(R \vee W)$
    2. $S \supset \sim(R \vee W)$ / $\sim S$
    3. $\sim S$ 1, 2, MT

(5) 1. $\sim C \supset (A \supset C)$
    2. $\sim C$ / $\sim A$
    3. $A \supset C$ 1, 2, MP
    4. $\sim A$ 2, 3, MT

(6) 1. $F \vee (D \supset T)$
    2. $\sim F$
    3. D / T
    4. $D \supset T$ 1, 2, DS
    5. T 3, 4, MP

(7) 1. $(K \cdot B) \vee (L \supset E)$
    2. $\sim(K \cdot B)$
    3. $\sim E$ / $\sim L$
    4. $L \supset E$ 1, 2, DS
    5. $\sim L$ 3, 4, MT

(8) 1. $P \supset (G \supset T)$
    2. $Q \supset (T \supset E)$
    3. P
    4. Q / $G \supset E$
    5. $G \supset T$ 1, 3, MP
    6. $T \supset E$ 2, 4, MP
    7. $G \supset E$ 5, 6, HS

(9) 1. $\sim W \supset [\sim W \supset (X \supset W)]$
    2. $\sim W$ / $\sim X$
    3. $\sim W \supset (X \supset W)$ 1, 2, MP
    4. $X \supset W$ 2, 3, MP
    5. $\sim X$ 2, 4, MT

Using the first four rules of inference, construct proofs of the following arguments.

(1) 1. $X \supset (Y \supset Z)$
    2. X
    3. Y / Z

(2) 1. $X \vee (Y \vee Z)$
    2. $\sim X$
    3. $\sim Y$ /Z

(3) 1. $X \vee \sim Y$
    2. $\sim X$
    3. $Z \supset Y$ / $\sim Z$

(4) 1. $X \supset (Y \vee Z)$
    2. $W \supset X$
    3. W
    4. $\sim Y$ / Z

(5) 1. $X \supset (\sim Y \supset \sim Z)$
    2. $\sim Y$
    3. $Y \vee X$ / $\sim Z$

(6) 1. $X \supset Y$
    2. $Y \supset Z$
    3. $\sim Z$ / $\sim X$

(7) 1. $X \supset (Y \supset Z)$
    2. $X \supset (Z \supset W)$
    3. $T \vee X$
    4. $\sim T$ / $Y \supset W$

(8) 1. $X \vee (Y \cdot Z)$
    2. $(Y \cdot Z) \supset W$
    3. $X \supset T$
    4. $\sim T$ /W

(9) 1. $\sim X \vee \sim Y$
    2. $\sim X \supset Z$
    3. $\sim Z$
    4. $Y \vee W$ /W

(10) 1. $X \supset (X \supset \sim Y)$
    2. $Y \vee \sim T$
    3. X
    4. $W \supset T$ / $\sim W$

7.2   RULES OF IMPLICATION II

In this section four additional rules of derivation are presented. As with the first four, they are valid argument forms.

5. $\dfrac{(p \supset q) \cdot (r \supset s)}{q \vee s}$ constructive dilemma (CD)

(with $p \vee r$ as the middle premise)

6. $\dfrac{p \cdot q}{p}$ simplification (Simp)

7. $\dfrac{\begin{array}{c} p \\ q \end{array}}{p \cdot q}$ conjunction (Conj)

8. $\dfrac{p}{p \vee q}$ addition (Add)

These rules may be used in connection with the first four rules. The first eight rules have the common characteristic that they must be applied to *whole lines* in proofs, and not merely to parts of lines. Without this restriction, the erroneous deduction

$$\frac{(p \cdot q) \supset r}{p \supset r}$$

might be thought to be justified by simplification, just to take one example. (The rules introduced later in this chapter, called rules of replacement, are not covered by this restriction.)

Sample Exercises from Exercise 7.2. Part II

(1) 1. $\sim M \supset Q$
2. $R \supset \sim T$
3. $\sim M \vee R$ / $Q \vee \sim T$
4. $(\sim M \supset Q) \cdot (R \supset \sim T)$ 1, 2, Conj
5. $Q \vee \sim T$ 3, 4, CD

(2) 1. $E \supset (A \cdot C)$
2. $A \supset (F \cdot E)$
3. E / F
4. $A \cdot C$ 1, 3, MP
5. A 4, Simp
6. $F \cdot E$ 2, 5, MP
7. F 6, Simp

(3) 1. $G \supset (S \cdot T)$
2. $(S \vee T) \supset J$
3. G / J
4. $S \cdot T$ 1, 3, MP
5. S 4, Simp
6. $S \vee T$ 5, Add
7. J 2, 6, MP

(4) 1. $(L \vee T) \supset (B \cdot G)$
2. $L \cdot (K \equiv R)$ / $L \cdot B$
3. L 2, Simp
4. $L \vee T$ 3, Add
5. $B \cdot G$ 1, 4, MP
6. B 5, Simp
7. $L \cdot B$ 3, 6, Conj

Additional Exercises for Section 7.2

Use the first eight rules of inference to construct proofs for the following arguments.

(1) 1. $(X \vee Y) \supset Z$
2. $(Z \vee T) \supset W$
3. X / W

(2) 1. $X \supset (Y \cdot Z)$
2. $Y \supset K$
3. W
4. $W \supset X$ / K

(3) 1. $X \supset (Y \vee Z)$
2. $Y \supset W$
3. $Z \supset K$
4. X / $W \vee K$

(4) 1. $X \supset Y$
    2. $(\sim X \vee W) \supset K$
    3. $\sim Y \cdot Z$ / $K \vee T$

(5) 1. $X \vee (Y \vee Z)$
    2. $\sim Y \cdot W$
    3. $\sim X \cdot T$ / $Z \vee T$

(6) 1. $(X \supset Y) \cdot (Z \supset W)$
    2. $(K \cdot L) \cdot M$
    3. $K \supset (X \vee Z)$ / $Y \vee W$

(7) 1. $(X \supset Y) \cdot L$
    2. $(Y \supset Z) \cdot M$
    3. $(X \supset Z) \supset [(X \supset Y) \supset W]$ / W

(8) 1. $(X \cdot Y) \vee (Z \cdot W)$
    2. $(X \cdot Y) \supset L$
    3. $\sim L \cdot M$
    4. $Z \supset (N \cdot O)$ / N

(9) 1. $(X \supset Y) \cdot Z$
    2. $X \cdot L$
    3. $(X \supset Y) \supset M$
    4. $(Y \cdot M) \supset (Z \cdot K)$ / $Z \vee W$

(10) 1. $X \supset P$
    2. $X \cdot R$
    3. $P \supset (Q \cdot S)$
    4. $(P \cdot Q) \supset (P \equiv Q)$ / $P \equiv Q$

(11) 1. $A \supset (B \supset C)$
    2. $A \cdot X$
    3. $B \cdot (Y \cdot Z)$ / $C \cdot A$

(12) 1. $(B \supset C) \supset A$
    2. $A \supset X$
    3. $\sim X \cdot Y$
    4. $D \supset (B \supset C)$ / $\sim A \cdot \sim D$

(13) 1. $(A \supset B) \cdot (C \supset D)$
    2. $(B \supset E) \cdot (F \supset G)$
    3. $(A \supset E) \supset (H \cdot I)$
    4. $H \supset J$ / $H \cdot J$

(14) 1. $(A \cdot B) \supset (C \vee D)$
    2. $C \supset E$
    3. $A \supset B$
    4. $A \cdot F$
    5. $(D \supset G) \cdot H$ / $(A \cdot B) \cdot (E \vee G)$

(15) 1. $A \supset B$
    2. $C \vee A$
    3. $C \supset D$
    4. $\sim D$ / $(B \cdot \sim C) \vee E$

7.3   RULES OF REPLACEMENT I

We saw in Sections 7.1 and 7.2 how valid argument forms may be used as rules of inference in natural deduction. Forms of logical equivalences may also be used as rules of inference. Every substitution instance of a form of logical equivalence is a logical equivalence; moreover, either one of a pair of logically equivalent expressions may be substituted for the other in a proof without loss of validity.

Five forms of logical equivalence are given in this section:

9. $\sim(p \cdot q)$ is logically equivalent to $(\sim p \vee \sim q)$.
     $\sim(p \vee q)$ is logically equivalent to $(\sim p \cdot \sim q)$.

These two statements are known as DeMorgan's Rule (DM).

10. $(p \vee q)$ is logically equivalent to $(q \vee p)$.
      $(p \cdot q)$ is logically equivalent to $(q \cdot p)$.

These two rules are known as commutativity (Com).

11. $[p \vee (q \vee r)]$ is logically equivalent to $[(p \vee q) \vee r]$.
      $[p \cdot (q \cdot r)]$ is logically equivalent to $[(p \cdot q) \cdot r]$.

These two rules are known as associativity (Assoc).

12. $[p \cdot (q \vee r)]$ is logically equivalent to $[(p \cdot q) \vee (p \cdot r)]$.
      $[p \vee (q \cdot r)]$ is logically equivalent to $[(p \vee q) \cdot (p \vee r)]$.

These two rules are known as distribution (Dist).

13. p is logically equivalent to $\sim\sim p$.

This is known as double negation (DN).

These and the remaining rules of replacement may be applied not only to whole lines in proofs—as the rules of implication must be—but to parts of lines as well. Thus, going from

$$(p \cdot q) \supset r$$

to

$$(q \cdot p) \supset r$$

by the rule of commutativity is quite proper.

Sample Exercises from Exercise 7.3. Part II

(1) 1. $(\sim M \supset P) \cdot (\sim N \supset Q)$
    2. $\sim(M \cdot N)$ $/ P \vee Q$
    3. $\sim M \vee \sim N$ 2, DM
    4. $P \vee Q$ 1, 3, CD

(2) 1. $J \vee (K \cdot L)$
    2. $\sim K$ $/ J$
    3. $\sim K \vee \sim L$ 2, Add
    4. $\sim(K \cdot L)$ 3, DM
    5. $(K \cdot L) \vee J$ 1, Com
    6. J 4, 5, DS

(3) 1. $R \supset \sim B$
   2. $D \vee R$
   3. B /D
   4. $\sim\sim B$ 3, DN
   5. $\sim R$ 1, 4, MT
   6. $R \vee D$ 2, Com
   7. D 5, 6, DS

(4) 1. $(O \vee M) \supset S$
   2. $\sim S$ / $\sim M$
   3. $\sim(O \vee M)$ 1, 2, MT
   4. $\sim O \cdot \sim M$ 3, DM
   5. $\sim M \cdot \sim O$ 4, Com
   6. $\sim M$ 5, Simp

Additional Exercises for Section 7.3

(1) 1. $\sim(X \cdot Y)$
   2. X
   3. $Y \vee Z$ /Z

(2) 1. $X \cdot (Y \vee Z)$
   2. $\sim(X \cdot Y)$
   3. $(Z \cdot X) \supset K$ /K

(3) 1. $\sim X \vee Y$
   2. $\sim Y \vee Z$
   3. $X \cdot W$ /$(X \cdot Y) \cdot Z$

(4) 1. $(X \vee Y) \supset Z$
   2. $\sim(Z \vee W)$ /$\sim Y$

(5) 1. $X \cdot (Y \cdot Z)$
   2. $(Y \cdot X) \supset (W \cdot T)$
   3. $(T \cdot Z) \supset L$ /$(Y \cdot W) \cdot Z$

(6) 1. $\sim X \supset T$
   2. $W \cdot \sim T$
   3. $(X \vee Y) \supset Z$ /$W \cdot Z$

(7) 1. $\sim X$
   2. $\sim(X \cdot Y) \supset \sim W$ /$\sim(W \cdot Z)$

(8) 1. $\sim(X \vee \sim X)$ /Y

(9) 1. X
   2. $(\sim Y \vee X) \supset Z$
   3. $\sim (X \cdot Z) \vee W$ /$(W \cdot X) \cdot Z$

(10) 1. $X \cdot \sim Z$
    2. $(Y \vee X) \supset \sim W$ /$\sim(Z \vee W)$

7.4   RULES OF REPLACEMENT II

The remaining five rules of replacement are:

14. $(p \supset q)$ is logically equivalent to $(\sim q \supset \sim p)$.

This rule is called transposition (Trans).

15. $(p \supset q)$ is logically equivalent to $(\sim p \lor q)$.

This rule is called material implication (Impl).

16. $(p \equiv q)$ is logically equivalent to $[(p \supset q) \cdot (q \supset p)]$.
$(p \equiv q)$ is logically equivalent to $[(p \cdot q) \lor (\sim p \cdot \sim q)]$.

These two rules together are known as material equivalence (Equiv).

17. $[(p \cdot q) \supset r]$ is logically equivalent to $[p \supset (q \supset r)]$.

This rule is known as exportation (Exp).

18. p is logically equivalent to $(p \lor p)$.
p is logically equivalent to $(p \cdot p)$.

These two rules are known as tautology (Taut).

Remember that all the rules of replacement may be applied to parts of lines as well as to whole lines.

Sample Exercises from Exercise 7.4. Part II

(1) 1. $(J \cdot R) \supset H$
    2. $(R \supset H) \supset M$
    3. $\sim(P \lor \sim J)$ $/M \cdot \sim P$
    4. $J \supset (R \supset H)$ 1, Exp
    5. $\sim P \cdot \sim\sim J$ 3, DM
    6. $\sim\sim J \cdot \sim P$ 5, Com
    7. $\sim\sim J$ 6, Simp
    8. J 7, DN
    9. $R \supset H$ 4, 8, MP
  10. M 2, 9, MP
  11. $\sim P$ 5, Simp
  12. $M \cdot \sim P$ 10, 11, Conj

(2) 1. $(B \supset G) \cdot (F \supset N)$
    2. $\sim(G \cdot N)$ $/ \sim(B \cdot F)$
    3. $\sim G \lor \sim N$ 2, DM
    4. $(\sim G \supset \sim B) \cdot (F \supset N)$ 1, Trans
    5. $(\sim G \supset \sim B) \cdot (\sim N \supset \sim F)$ 4, Trans
    6. $\sim B \lor \sim F$ 3, 5, CD
    7. $\sim(B \cdot F)$ 6, DM

(3) 1. T $/ S \supset T$
    2. $T \lor \sim S$ 1, Add
    3. $\sim S \lor T$ 2, Com
    4. $S \supset T$ 3, Impl

(4) 1. $\sim(U \cdot W) \supset X$
2. $U \supset \sim U$ / $\sim(U \vee \sim X)$
3. $\sim U \vee \sim U$ 2, Impl
4. $\sim U$ 3, Taut
5. $\sim U \vee \sim W$ 4, Add
6. $\sim(U \cdot W)$ 5, DM
7. X 1, 6, MP
8. $\sim\sim X$ 7, DN
9. $\sim U \cdot \sim\sim X$ 4, 8, Conj
10. $\sim(U \vee \sim X)$ 9, DM

Additional Exercises for Section 7.4

(1) 1. X
  2. $(Y \supset X) \supset Z$ /$X \cdot Z$

(2) 1. $X \supset Y$
  2. $(Y \vee \sim X) \supset (Y \supset Z)$ / $\sim Z \supset \sim X$

(3) 1. X
  2. Y /$X \equiv Y$

(4) 1. X
  2. $X \supset \sim Y$ /$X \equiv \sim Y$

(5) 1. $X \supset Y$
  2. $X \supset Z$ /$X \supset (Y \cdot Z)$

(6) 1. $X \supset (Y \cdot Z)$ /$(X \supset Y) \cdot (X \supset Z)$

(7) 1. $X \supset Z$
  2. $Y \supset Z$ /$(X \vee Y) \supset Z$

(8) 1. $(X \vee Y) \supset Z$ /$(X \supset Z) \cdot (Y \supset Z)$

(9) 1. $X \supset (X \cdot Y)$
  2. $[(X \cdot Y) \vee (\sim X \cdot Y)] \supset Y$ /$Y \supset Y$

(10) 1. $(X \cdot Y) \supset X$
  2. Y
  3. $(X \supset X) \supset X$ /$X \cdot Y$

(11) 1. $A \supset (B \vee C)$
  2. $\sim B$ /$A \supset C$

(12) 1. $A \supset (B \vee C)$
  2. $B \supset C$ /$A \supset C$

(13) 1. $(A \supset B) \supset (B \supset A)$ /$B \supset A$

(14) 1. A
  2. $\sim B$ / $\sim(A \equiv B)$

(15) 1. $\sim(A \equiv B)$
  2. A / $\sim B$

(16) 1. ~$(A \equiv B)$ / ~$A \equiv B$

(17) 1. ~$(A \equiv B)$ /$A \equiv$ ~B

(18) 1. ~$(A \supset B)$
     2. ~$(C \supset D)$ / ~$(A \supset D)$

(19) 1. ~$(A \supset B)$
     2. ~$(B \supset C)$ /$A \supset C$

(20) 1. ~$(A \equiv B)$
     2. ~$(B \equiv C)$ /$A \equiv C$

7.5   CONDITIONAL PROOF

Our system of eighteen rules, although powerful, is still not complete; that is, there are valid arguments for which our rules do not permit the construction of a proof. Two examples of such valid arguments are

$$X // Y \vee \sim Y$$

and

$$X \supset Y // X \supset (X \cdot Y)$$

With the addition of *conditional proof* to our system, however, the rules become complete: a proof may be constructed for any valid argument of propositional logic.

The fundamental idea of conditional proof may be viewed as an analog or extension of the rule of exportation. Recall that according to this rule $p \supset (q \supset r)$ is logically equivalent to $(p \cdot q) \supset r$. Analogously, it is a fact that an argument

$$p // q \supset r$$

is valid if and only if the argument

$$p / q // r$$

is valid. More generally, for any number of premises $p_1, p_2, \ldots, p_n$ the argument

$$p_1 / p_2 / \ldots / p_n // q \supset r$$

is valid if and only if the argument

$$p_1 / p_2 / \ldots / p_n / q // r$$

is valid. This implies that to prove an argument with a conditional conclusion $q \supset r$ valid, it is sufficient to assume the antecedent q of that conditional and then from this assumption, together with the premises of the argument, deduce the consequent r of that conditional. The process of carrying out this sort of deduction is called conditional proof (CP).

Conditional proof may be diagrammatically represented in this way:

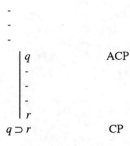

q	ACP
-	
-	
-	
r	
$q \supset r$	CP

In this diagram, q is the assumption. (Any proposition may be assumed in this way at any time.) The indented lines (called the *scope* of the assumption) all follow from the premises only conditionally (that is, with the help of the assumption). At the nonindented line $q \supset r$, the assumption is said to be *discharged*. That is, $q \supset r$ follows unconditionally from the original premises alone. (An assumption may be discharged at any time, provided that the diagrammatic format is followed.)

Sample Exercises from Exercise 7.5. Part I

(1)
1. $N \supset O$
2. $N \supset P$ /$N \supset (O \cdot P)$
   3. N ACP
   4. O 1, 3, MP
   5. P 2, 3, MP
   6. $O \cdot P$ 4, 5, Conj
7. $N \supset (O \cdot P)$ 3-6, CP

(2)
1. $F \supset E$
2. $(F \cdot E) \supset R$ /$F \supset R$
   3. F ACP
   4. E 1, 3, MP
   5. $F \cdot E$ 3, 4, Conj
   6. R 2, 5, MP
7. $F \supset R$ 3-6, CP

(3)
1. $G \supset T$
2. $(T \vee S) \supset K$ /$G \supset K$
   3. G ACP
   4. T 1, 3, MP
   5. $T \vee S$ 4, Add
   6. K 2, 5, MP
7. $G \supset K$ 3–6, CP

(4)
1. $(G \vee H) \supset (S \cdot T)$
2. $(T \vee U) \supset (C \cdot D)$ /$G \supset C$
   3. G ACP
   4. $G \vee H$ 3, Add
   5. $S \cdot T$ 1, 4, MP
   6. $T \cdot S$ 5, Com
   7. T 6, Simp
   8. $T \vee U$ 7, Add
   9. $C \cdot D$ 2, 8, MP
   10. C 9, Simp
11. $G \supset C$ 3–10, CP

Additional Exercises for Section 7.5

Use CP in proving the following arguments valid.

(1) 1. $(X \vee Y) \supset (Z \cdot W)$ /$Y \supset W$

(2) 1. $(X \vee Y) \supset [(Z \vee W) \supset R]$ /$(X \cdot W) \supset R$

(3) 1. $X \supset Y$
    2. $Z \supset W$ $\qquad\qquad\qquad$ $/(X \lor Z) \supset (Y \lor W)$

(4) 1. $X \supset Y$
    2. $Z \supset W$ $\qquad\qquad\qquad$ $/(X \cdot Z) \supset (Y \cdot W)$

(5) 1. $(X \lor Y) \supset [(Z \lor W) \supset R]$ $\qquad$ $/X \supset (Z \supset R)$

(6) 1. $X \supset Y$
    2. $Z \supset W$ $\qquad\qquad\qquad$ $/(\sim Y \cdot \sim W) \supset (\sim X \cdot \sim Z)$

(7) 1. $X \supset (Y \cdot Z)$
    2. $Z \supset (X \cdot W)$ $\qquad\qquad$ $/X \equiv Z$

(8) 1. $(X \lor Y) \supset Z$
    2. $(\sim X \lor \sim L) \supset (\sim Z \cdot \sim W)$ $\qquad$ $/X \equiv Z$

(9) 1. $X \supset Y$
    2. $Z \supset Y$ $\qquad\qquad\qquad$ $/(X \lor Z) \supset Y$

(10) 1. $\sim(X \cdot Y)$
     2. $\sim[Z \cdot (Y \lor W)]$ $\qquad\qquad$ $/Y \supset (\sim X \cdot \sim Z)$

7.6   INDIRECT PROOF

Indirect proof, or proof by *reductio ad absurdum,* is a technique familiar to many students of plane geometry. It consists in assuming the *opposite* of what is to be proved and then deriving a contradiction from this assumption together with the other premises. When a contradiction is shown, it may be concluded that what was originally to be proved has been proved.

Indirect proof may be represented as a special application of conditional proof in the following way. Suppose some conclusion q is to be proved from some premises; suppose also that by assuming the opposite of q (that is, $\sim q$), a contradiction (for example, $r \cdot \sim r$) can be deduced. We may represent this situation as follows:

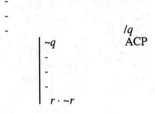

We may continue deducing as follows:

$$
\begin{array}{lll}
& r & \text{Simp} \\
& \sim r \cdot r & \text{Com} \\
& \sim r & \text{Simp} \\
& r \vee q & \text{Add} \\
& q & \text{DS} \\
\sim q \supset q & & \text{CP} \\
\sim\sim q \vee q & & \text{Impl} \\
q \vee q & & \text{DN} \\
q & & \text{Taut}
\end{array}
$$

This representation shows that an indirect proof is in effect a conditional proof of a particular sort, in which deduction is carried out right on through the contradiction. It would be unnecessarily repetitive to insist that every time this technique is employed the steps of the deduction that follow the contradiction should be explicitly listed. Accordingly, we may employ the following format for indirect proof (IP):

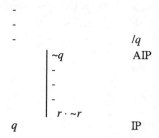

A slightly different but obviously equivalent format for indirect proof is:

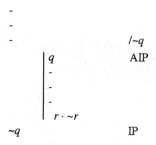

In employing these formats, we can use any proposition in the place of r.

Sample Exercises from Exercise 7.6. Part I

$$
\begin{array}{lll}
(1) \; 1. & (S \vee T) \supset \sim S & / \sim S \\
\quad\; 2. & \sim\sim S & \text{AIP} \\
\quad\; 3. & S & 2, \text{DN} \\
\quad\; 4. & S \vee T & 3, \text{Add} \\
\quad\; 5. & \sim S & 1, 4, \text{MP} \\
\quad\; 6. & S \cdot \sim S & 3, 5, \text{Conj} \\
\quad\; 7. & \sim S & 2\text{--}6, \text{IP}
\end{array}
$$

or:

$$
\begin{array}{lll}
\quad\;\; 2. & S & \text{AIP} \\
\quad\;\; 3. & S \lor T & 2,\ \text{Add} \\
\quad\;\; 4. & \sim\! S & 1,\ 3,\ \text{MP} \\
\quad\;\; 5. & S \cdot \sim\! S & 2,\ 4,\ \text{Conj} \\
6. & \sim\! S & 2\text{–}5,\ \text{IP}
\end{array}
$$

(2)
$$
\begin{array}{lll}
1. & (K \supset K) \supset R & \\
2. & (R \lor M) \supset N & /N \\
\quad\;\; 3. & \sim\! N & \text{AIP} \\
\quad\;\; 4. & \sim\!(R \lor M) & 2,\ 3,\ \text{MT} \\
\quad\;\; 5. & \sim\! R \cdot \sim\! M & 4,\ \text{DM} \\
\quad\;\; 6. & \sim\! R & 5,\ \text{Simp} \\
\quad\;\; 7. & \sim\!(K \supset K) & 1,\ 6,\ \text{MT} \\
\quad\;\; 8. & \sim\!(\sim\! K \lor K) & 7,\ \text{Impl} \\
\quad\;\; 9. & \sim\!\sim\! K \cdot \sim\! K & 8,\ \text{Dist} \\
\quad 10. & K \cdot \sim\! K & \text{DN} \\
11. & N & 3\text{–}10,\ \text{IP}
\end{array}
$$

Additional Exercises for Section 7.6

Use IP in proving the following arguments valid.

(1) 1. $X \,/\, Y \lor \sim\! Y$

(2) 1. $X \cdot Y$
    2. $Y \supset Z$ $/Z \lor W$

(3) 1. $X \supset Y$
    2. $Y \supset \sim\! Y$ $/\!\sim\! X$

(4) 1. $\sim\! X \supset X$
    2. $X \supset Y$
    3. $\sim\! Y \lor Z$ $/Z$

(5) 1. $X \supset Y$
    2. $Z \supset W$
    3. $\sim\! Y \lor T$
    4. $\sim\! U \supset \sim\! W$
    5. $\sim\! X \supset Z$ $/T \lor U$

7.7   PROVING LOGICAL TRUTHS

The devices of conditional proof and indirect proof furnish a new technique (or, more properly: a *pair* of techniques) for showing that certain propositions are logical truths—that is, tautologies.

A proposition of the form $p \supset q$ is a tautology if and only if the argument $p \,/\, q$ is a valid argument. Thus, in order to show that $p \supset q$ is a tautology, it is sufficient to assume p and then to derive q validly from p. This process may be represented in the format of CP in an obvious way:

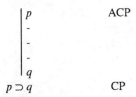

p	ACP
-	
-	
-	
q	
$p \supset q$	CP

Moreover, a proposition p is a tautology if and only if $\sim p$ is a self-contradiction, and any proposition is a self-contradiction if and only if an explicit contradiction—a proposition of the form $q \cdot \sim q$—may be derived validly from it. Thus, in order to show p to be a tautology, it is sufficient to assume p and to derive an explicit contradiction from it. This process may be represented in the format of IP as follows:

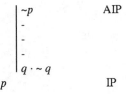

$\sim p$	AIP
-	
-	
-	
$q \cdot \sim q$	
p	IP

In effect, then, a proposition may be shown tautologous by deriving it from no premises at all, by means of CP or IP. In such a derivation it is convenient to represent the proposition that is to be shown tautologous as the conclusion of an argument having no premises.

Sample Exercises from Exercise 7.7

(1) $/ P \supset [(P \supset Q) \supset Q]$

1.	P	ACP
2.	$P \supset Q$	ACP
3.	Q	1, 2, MP
4.	$(P \supset Q) \supset Q$	2, 3, CP
5.	$P \supset [(P \supset Q) \supset Q]$	1–4, CP

(2) $/ (\sim P \supset Q) \vee (P \supset R)$

1.	$\sim[(\sim P \supset Q) \vee (P \supset P)]$	AIP
2.	$\sim(\sim P \supset Q) \cdot \sim(P \supset R)$	1, DM
3.	$\sim(\sim\sim P \vee Q) \cdot \sim(P \supset R)$	2, Impl
4.	$\sim(\sim\sim P \vee Q)$	3, Simp
5.	$\sim(P \vee Q)$	4, DN
6.	$\sim P \cdot \sim Q$	5, DM
7.	$\sim P$	6, Simp
8.	$\sim \quad (P \supset R) \cdot \sim(\sim\sim P \vee Q)$	3, Com
9.	$\sim(P \supset R)$	8, Simp
10.	$\sim(\sim P \vee R)$	9, Impl
11.	$\sim\sim P \cdot \sim R$	10, DM
12.	$\sim\sim P$	11, Simp
13.	P	12, DN
14.	$P \cdot \sim P$	7, 13, Conj
15.	$(\sim P \supset Q) \vee (P \supset R)$	1–14, IP

Additional Exercises for Section 7.7

Use CP or IP to show the following propositions to be tautologies.

(1) $P \supset [P \cdot (Q \vee \sim Q)]$

(2) $P \supset [\sim P \supset (P \vee P)]$

(3) $[(P \supset Q) \supset P] \supset P$

(4) $(P \supset Q) \vee (P \cdot \sim Q)$

(5) $(P \vee Q) \vee [\sim P \cdot (Q \supset \sim Q)]$

8
PREDICATE LOGIC

8.1   SYMBOLS AND TRANSLATION

In *predicate logic* the fundamental component of representation of propositions is the *predicate*. We shall use upper case letters to stand for predicates. Thus, the letter A might stand for the predicate of being altruistic. With this symbolization, the proposition "Socrates is altruistic" could be represented as "A (Socrates)." If we use a lower case letter s to stand for Socrates and omit the really unnecessary parentheses, the same proposition can be represented as As. If a lower case p is used to stand for Plato, then the proposition "Plato is altruistic" can be represented by Ap. In general, we shall allocate the lower case letters of the alphabet—with the exception of x, y, and z—as symbols to stand for individuals; they are called *individual constants*.

These conventions of predicate logic can be combined with those of propositional logic in a straightforward way. Thus, the proposition "If Socrates is altruistic, then Plato is altruistic" can be represented as As ⊃ Ap; the proposition "Socrates is altruistic but Plato is not" can be represented as As · ~Ap, and so on.

Representing quantified propositions in predicate logic requires a little more symbolic apparatus. First, we require the idea of an *individual variable.* We shall allocate the lower case letters x, y, and z for use as individual variables. Such variables, which are similar to the variables used in algebra, may be thought of as *ranging over* absolutely all individuals—as referring indifferently to anything at all. Individual variables figure into symbolizations in two ways: they are part of *logical quantifiers,* and they are attached to predicates just as individual constants are attached to predicates. These are two logical quantifiers, the universal quantifier and the existential quantifier. The *universal quantifier,* written (x) and read "for any x," is used to express a universal logical quantification. For example, (x)Ax says that for any x, x is altruistic or, in other words, that everything is altruistic. The *existential quantifier,* written (∃x) and read as "there exists an x such that," is used to express a particular logical quantification. For example, (∃x)Ax says that there exists an x such that x is altruistic or, in other words, that something (at least one thing) is altruistic. The existential quantifier may also be read as "for some x." Accordingly, (∃x)Ax may also be read as "for some x, x is altruistic."

More generally, the universal and existential quantifiers can be attached to any significant context containing variables. Thus, (x)(Ax ∨ ~Ax) means that everything is either altruistic or not altruistic. This fact means that we can, for example, symbolize the four standard types of categorical propositions with the apparatus of predicate logic. The **A** proposition, "All S are P," means (in the modern interpretation) "If anything is an S then it is a P." In other words, it means "For any x, if x is an S then X is a P." Thus, the **A** proposition may be symbolized as:

$$(x)(Sx \supset Px)$$

Similarly, the **E** proposition (in the modern interpretation) may be symbolized:

$$(x)(Sx \supset \sim Px)$$

The **I** proposition, on either the modern or the traditional interpretation, becomes:

$$(\exists x)(Sx \cdot Px)$$

The **O** proposition, on either the modern or the traditional interpretation, becomes:

$$(\exists x)(Sx \cdot {\sim}Px)$$

With the apparatus of predicate logic, a great many quantified propositions can be expressed. The test contains many examples of this usage of predicate logic.

Sample Exercises from Exercise 8.1

1. Elaine is a chemist.

   Letting *e* stand for Elaine, we get:

   $$Ce$$

2. All maples are trees.

   $$(x)(Mx \supset Tx)$$

3. Some grapes are sour.

   $$(\exists x)(Gx \cdot Sx)$$

4. No novels are biographies.

   $$(x)(Nx \supset {\sim}Bx)$$

5. Some holidays are not relaxing.

   $$(\exists x)(Hx \cdot {\sim}Rx)$$

6. If Gertrude is correct, then the Taj Mahal is made of marble.

   Letting *g* stand for Gertrude and *t* for the Taj Mahal, we get:

   $$Cg \supset Mt$$

7. Gertrude is not correct only if the Taj Mahal is made of granite.

   $${\sim}Cg \supset Gt$$

Additional Exercises for Section 8.1

Translate the following statements into the symbolism of predicate logic using the indicated letters as predicates.

1. Snakes are reptiles.   (S, R)

2. If a snake is a rattler, then it is poisonous.   (S, R, P)

3. If a snake is poisonous, then it is either a rattler or a cobra.   (S, P, R, C)

4. Only poisonous snakes are rattlers.   (P, S, R)

5. Some poisonous snakes are rattlers.   (P, S, R)

6. A rattler is poisonous only if it is a snake.   (*R, P, S*)

7. A cobra is a rattler if and only if it is not poisonous.   (*C, R, P*)

8. Some cobras are poisonous only if they are snakes.   (*C, P, S*)

9. A poisonous snake is in the zoo.   (*P, S, Z*)

10. A poisonous snake is a deadly creature.   (*P, S, D, C*)

8.2   USING THE RULES OF INFERENCE

In predicate logic we often wish to make use of the deductive apparatus of propositional logic in order to construct proofs or derivations of valid arguments. For example, we might want to invoke simplification to prove the validity of the argument $(x)(Ax \cdot Bx) / (x)Ax$. But many of the rules of inference of propositional logic (such as simplification) may be applied only to whole lines in a proof. Thus, we need rules for dropping initial quantifiers from quantified propositions. If we remove quantifiers in the course of constructing a proof, we also eventually need to add initial quantifiers in order to complete the proof, so we need rules for doing this, also. Thus, we need rules for both removing initial quantifiers (*instantiating*) and introducing initial quantifiers (*generalizing*).

If the quantifier (x) is removed from $(x)(Ax \cdot Bx)$, the result is $Ax \cdot Bx$. Since x is a variable and not a constant, $Ax \cdot Bx$ makes no statement at all. (It is to be contrasted with, for instance, $Ac \cdot Bc$, which says of some named individual c that it is both an A and a B.) $Ax \cdot Bx$ is what logicians call a *propositional function* or a *statement function.* Even though it makes no statement, its significance in the context of a proof may be viewed as corresponding to the statement "Take any arbitrarily selected individual: *it* is both A and B." Clearly this statement does follow validly from $(x)(Ax \cdot Bx)$, and it also clearly entails $(x)(Ax \cdot Bx)$. This perspective on propositional functions helps explain *universal instantiation* (dropping a universal quantifier) and *universal generalization* (adding a universal quantifier).

We have now seen that we can universally instantiate to variables and universally generalize from them. But how about constants? Well, if $(x)(Ax \cdot Bx)$ is true and c is some named individual, then clearly $Ac \cdot Bc$ is true. So we can universally instantiate to constants. Notice, however, that we cannot universally generalize from a constant: Going from $Ac \cdot Bc$ to $(x)(Ax \cdot Bx)$ is clearly invalid. Thus, we can universally generalize only from variables, never from constants. We are now in a position to state the rules for universal instantiation (UI) and universal generalization (UG).

Let us use the symbol $\mathcal{F}x$ to denote any propositional function in x, like Ax, $Ax \cdot Bx$, $Ax \supset \sim Bx$, and so on. $\mathcal{F}y$ will denote the result of replacing every unquantified-over occurrence of x in $\mathcal{F}x$ by the variable y. (Here y may be, but need not be, x.) And $\mathcal{F}c$ will denote the result of replacing every unquantified-over occurrence of x in $\mathcal{F}x$ by the constant c. The UI can be diagrammatically represented as:

UI $\dfrac{(x)\mathcal{F}x}{\mathcal{F}y}$ or $\dfrac{(x)\mathcal{F}x}{\mathcal{F}c}$

Here y is *any variable* and c is *any constant.* Similarly, UG can be represented as:

UG $\dfrac{\mathcal{F}y}{(x)\mathcal{F}x}$

Here y is *any variable* (not a constant). In employing UG, one must be careful to replace *all* the occurrences of y in $\mathcal{F}y$ by occurrences of x in $\mathcal{F}x$.

In *existential instantiation* (EI) we want to remove an existential quantifier. It is clearly invalid to conclude from, say, $(\exists x)(Ax \cdot Bx)$ to $Ax \cdot Bx$, so we cannot existentially instantiate to a variable. In instantiating existentially, the idea is that from the claim that there is *something* that is both an *A* and a *B* we should be able to conclude that *some* definite thing, even if we do not know what thing it is, is both an *A* and a *B*. And we can *name* it—the thing claimed to exist—with a name, say *c*. Then we can conclude that $Ac \cdot Bc$ is true. In existentially instantiating, then, we are in effect picking a name for some individual, only it is an individual whose identity we do not know. Thus, we can existentially instantiate only to a constant. Moreover, the constant we pick as the instantial letter must be a *new* one; that is, it must not have occurred previously in the proof. Otherwise, we would be concluding too much—not merely (and legitimately) that *some* definite thing, which we name, say *c*, is both *A* and *B*, but also (and illegitimately) that this thing is identical with some object to which we have already referred. Thus, the rule for EI can be presented as:

$$\text{EI} \quad \frac{(\exists x)\mathscr{F}x}{\mathscr{F}c}$$

Here *c* is *any constant that has not previously occurred* in the proof.

In *existential generalization* (EG) we want to add an existential quantifier. Clearly it is legitimate to go from $Ac \cdot Bc$ to $(\exists x)(Ax \cdot Bx)$. But moreover, on the mere assumption that anything at all exists, we should also be able to go from $Ay \cdot By$ to $(\exists x)(Ax \cdot Bx)$. So the rule for EG can be represented as:

$$\text{EG} \quad \frac{\mathscr{F}c}{(\exists x)\mathscr{F}x} \quad \text{or} \quad \frac{\mathscr{F}y}{(\exists x)\mathscr{F}x}$$

Here *c* is *any constant* and *y* is *any variable*. In employing EG one need not be careful, as one does need to be careful in employing UG, to replace *all* the occurrences of *y* in $\mathscr{F}y$ (alternatively: of *c* in $\mathscr{F}c$) by occurrences of *x* in $\mathscr{F}x$. In fact, in order to comply with the rule, one must do no more than replace *one or more* of the occurrences of *y* in $\mathscr{F}y$ (alternatively: of *c* in $\mathscr{F}c$) by occurrences of *x* in $\mathscr{F}x$. This feature of EG sharply distinguishes the application of this rule from the application of UG.

In constructing proofs in predicate logic, the typical procedure involves three stages. First, premises are instantiated where necessary. Second, the techniques of propositional logic are applied. Third, the results of the second stage are appropriately generalized to reach the conclusion. There are a number of examples of this procedure in the text.

Note that when both existential and universal instantiations are to be done in a proof, the existential instantiations should be performed first; otherwise, the restriction on EI might make it impossible to apply the techniques of propositional logic (see the text for further elucidation of this point). Note also that the rules for dropping and adding quantifiers apply only to whole lines. It is illegitimate to go from, say, $(x)Ax \supset (\exists x)Bx$ to $Ay \supset (\exists x)Bx$, or from $\sim(x)Ax$ to $\sim Ay$. It is also illegitimate to go from, say, $Ac \cdot Bc$ to $(\exists x)Ax \cdot Bc$.

Sample Exercises from Exercise 8.2. Part I

(1)	1.	$(x)(Ax \supset Bx)$	
	2.	$(x)(Bx \supset Cx)$	$/(x)(Ax \supset Cx)$
	3.	$Ay \supset By$	1, UI
	4.	$By \supset Cy$	2, UI
	5.	$Ay \supset Cy$	3, 4, HS
	6.	$(x)(Ax \supset Cx)$	5, UG

(2) 1. $(x)(Bx \supset Cx)$
   2. $(\exists x)(Ax \cdot Bx)$ $/ (\exists x)(Ax \cdot Cx)$
   3. $Ac \cdot Bc$ 2, EI
   4. Ac 3, Simp
   5. $Bc \cdot Ac$ 3, Com
   6. Bc 5, Simp
   7. $Bc \supset Cc$ 1, UI
   8. Cc 6, 7, MP
   9. $Ac \cdot Cc$ 4, 8, Conj
   10. $(\exists x)(Ax \cdot Cx)$ 9, EG

(3) 1. $(x)(Ax \supset Bx)$
   2. $\sim Bm$ $/ (\exists x)\sim Ax$
   3. $Am \supset Bm$ 1, UI
   4. $\sim Am$ 2, 3, MT
   5. $(\exists x)\sim Ax$ 4, EG

(4) 1. $(x)[Ax \supset (Bx \lor Cx)]$
   2. $Ag \cdot \sim Bg$ $/Cg$
   3. Ag 2, Simp
   4. $\sim Bg \cdot Ag$ 2, Com
   5. $\sim Bg$ 4, Simp
   6. $Ag \supset (Bg \lor Cg)$ 1, UI
   7. $Bg \lor Cg$ 3, 6, MP
   8. Cg 5, 7, DS

Additional Exercises for Section 8.2

Using the rules for dropping and adding quantifiers and the rules of inference of propositional logic, but without using CP or IP, construct proofs for the following arguments.

(1) 1. $(x)(Ax \supset Bx)$
   2. $(x)(Bx \supset Cx)$
   3. $(x)(Cx \supset Dx)$ $/(x)(\sim Dx \supset \sim Ax)$

(2) 1. $(x)(Ax \cdot Bx)$
   2. $(\exists x)Ax \supset (\exists x)Cx$ $/ (\exists x)Cx$

(3) 1. $(\exists x)(Ax \cdot Bx)$ $/ (\exists x)Ax \cdot (\exists x)Bx$

(4) 1. $(x)Ax \lor (x)Bx$
   2. $(x)Ax \supset (x)Cx$
   3. $\sim(x)Cx$ $/ (\exists x)Bx$

(5) 1. $(x)(Ax \lor Bx)$
   2. $(x) \sim Ax$
   3. $(\exists x)Bx \supset (x)Cx$ $/(x)(Cx \lor Dx)$

(6) 1. $(x)[(Ax \cdot Bx) \lor Cx]$
   2. $(\exists x)\sim Bx$ $/ (\exists x)Cx$

(7) 1. $(x)[Ax \supset (Bx \supset Cx)]$
   2. $(\exists x)(Ax \lor Dx)$
   3. $(x) \sim Dx$
   4. $(x)Bx$ $/ (\exists x)Cx$

(8) 1. $(x)(Ax \supset Bx)$
    2. $(x)Ax$ $/(x)Bx$

(9) 1. $(\exists x)(Ax \cdot Bx)$
    2. $(x)[Bx \supset (Dx \cdot Ex)]$
    3. $(x)(Ex \supset {\sim}Fx)$ $/(\exists x){\sim}Fx$

(10) 1. $(x)(Ax \supset Bx)$
     2. $(x)({\sim}Bx \vee Cx)$
     3. $(\exists x)Ax$
     4. $(x) {\sim} Cx$ $/(x)Ax$

8.3   CHANGE OF QUANTIFIER RULES

Propositions with negation signs before quantifiers may easily be changed to logically equivalent propositions without negation signs before their quantifiers: The negation sign is moved from its initial position to the propositional function governed by the quantifier and the quantifier is changed to its opposite. This may be expressed in the following rules, called collectively the *change of quantifier rules* (CQ).

CQ ${\sim}(x)\mathcal{F}x$ is logically equivalent to $(\exists x) {\sim}\mathcal{F}x$
                 ${\sim}(x) {\sim}\mathcal{F}x$ is logically equivalent to $(\exists x)\mathcal{F}x$
                 ${\sim}(\exists x)\mathcal{F}x$ is logically equivalent to $(x) {\sim}\mathcal{F}x$
                 ${\sim}(\exists x) {\sim}\mathcal{F}x$ is logically equivalent to $(x)\mathcal{F}x$

These rules may, of course, be used in either direction, and they need not be applied only to whole lines.

Sample Exercises from Exercise 8.3. Part I

(1) 1. $(x)Ax \supset (\exists x)Bx$
    2. $(x){\sim}Bx$ $/(\exists x){\sim}Ax$
    3. ${\sim}(\exists x){\sim}{\sim}Bx$ 2, CQ
    4. ${\sim}(\exists x)Bx$ 3, DN
    5. ${\sim}(x)Ax$ 1, 4, MT
    6. $(\exists x){\sim}Ax$ 5, CQ

(2) 1. $(\exists x){\sim}Ax \vee (\exists x){\sim}Bx$
    2. $(x)Bx$ $/{\sim}(x)Ax$
    3. ${\sim}(\exists x){\sim}Bx$ 2, CQ
    4. $(\exists x){\sim}Bx \vee (\exists x) {\sim}Ax$ 1, Com
    5. $(\exists x){\sim}Ax$ 3, 4, DS
    6. ${\sim}(x){\sim}{\sim}Ax$ 5, CQ
    7. ${\sim}(x)Ax$ 6, DN

(3) 1. ${\sim}(\exists x)Ax$ $/(x)(Ax \supset Bx)$
    2. $(x) {\sim} Ax$ 1, CQ
    3. ${\sim} Ax$ 2, UI
    4. ${\sim}Ax \vee Bx$ 3, Add
    5. $Ax \supset Bx$ 4, Impl
    6. $(x)(Ax \supset Bx)$ 5, UG

8.4 CONDITIONAL AND INDIRECT PROOF

The use of conditional and indirect proof in predicate logic is basically the same as for propositional logic. The format is entirely the same.

When the antecedent and consequent of the proposition to be established by conditional proof are whole propositions—not propositional functions—the use of conditional or indirect proof presents no special problems. Sometimes, however, it is desirable to employ conditional proof in such a way that the antecedent of the conditional to be established is not a whole statement but rather a statement function. For example, in order to prove valid the argument $(x)[Ax \supset (Bx \cdot Cx)] / (x)(Ax \supset Bx)$, one would like to be able to assume Ax, to deduce Bx from this assumption and the premise, and then to discharge the assumption and universally generalize to the conclusion. In using CP in this manner, however, we must be careful to observe a special restriction on universal generalization: *In the scope of an assumption, UG must not be used to generalize on a variable that occurs in that assumption ungoverned by a quantifier.*

The basic reason for this restriction on UG is that we do not want to be able to derive lines like $Ax \supset (x)Ax$ merely by assuming Ax. To allow such lines is tantamount to allowing obviously invalid arguments to be proved as valid. For example, consider the argument $(\exists x)Ax / (x)Ax$. It is obviously invalid. But without the restriction on UG, we could derive its validity easily, as follows:

1.	$(\exists x)Ax$	$/(x)Ax$
	2. $\sim Ax$	ACP
	3. $(x)\sim Ax$	2, UG (invalid)
4.	$\sim Ax \supset (x)\sim Ax$	2-3, CP
5.	$\sim(x)\sim Ax$	1, CQ
6.	$\sim\sim Ax$	4, 5, MT
7.	Ax	6, DN
8.	$(x)Ax$	7, UG

Since indirect proof is only a special case of conditional proof, the restriction on UG also extends to IP. A variable is not to be generalized upon by UG inside the scope of an IP assumption if that variable occurs in that assumption ungoverned by a quantifier. Here is an example of the derivation of the same invalid argument as above by a faulty use of UG inside the scope of an assumption introduced by IP:

1.	$(\exists x)Ax$	$/ (x)Ax$
	2. $\sim Ax$	AIP
	3. $(x)\sim Ax$	2, UG (invalid)
	4. $\sim(\exists x)Ax$	3, CQ
	5. $(\exists x)Ax \cdot \sim(\exists x)Ax$	1, 4, Conj
6.	Ax	2-5, IP
7.	$(x)Ax$	6, UG

Sample Exercises from Exercise 8.4. Part I

(1) 1. $(x)(Ax \supset Bx)$
    2. $(x)(Ax \supset Cx)$ $/ (x)[Ax \supset (Bx \cdot Cx)]$
       3. Ax ACP
       4. $Ax \supset Bx$ 1, UI
       5. $Ax \supset Cx$ 2, UI
       6. Bx 3, 4, MP
       7. Cx 3, 5, MP
       8. $Bx \cdot Cx$ 6, 7, Conj
      9. $Ax \supset (Bx \cdot Cx)$ 3-8, CP
   10. $(x)[Ax \supset (Bx \cdot Cx)]$ 9, UG

(2) 1. $(\exists x)Ax \supset (\exists x)(Bx \cdot Cx)$
    2. $(\exists x)(Cx \vee Dx) \supset (x)Ex$ $/(x)(Ax \supset Ex)$
       3. Ax ACP
       4. $(\exists x)Ax$ 3, EG
       5. $(\exists x)(Bx \cdot Cx)$ 1, 4, MP
       6. $Bc \cdot Cc$ 5, EI
       7. $Cc \cdot Bc$ 6, Com
       8. Cc 7, Simp
       9. $Cc \vee Dc$ 8, Add
      10. $(\exists x)(Cx \vee Dx)$ 9, EG
      11. $(x)Ex$ 2, 10, MP
      12. Ex 11, UI
   13. $Ax \supset Ex$ 3-12, CP
   14. $(x)(Ax \supset Ex)$ 13, UG

(3) 1. $(\exists x)Ax \supset (\exists x)(Bx \cdot Cx)$
    2. $\sim (\exists x)Cx$ $/(x) \sim Ax$
       3. $\sim(x)\sim Ax$ AIP
       4. $(\exists x)Ax$ 3, CQ
       5. $(\exists x)(Bx \cdot Cx)$ 1, 4, MP
       6. $Bc \cdot Cc$ 5, EI
       7. $Cc \cdot Bc$ 6, Com
       8. Cc 7, Simp
       9. $(\exists x)Cx$ 8, EG
      10. $(\exists x)Cx \cdot \sim(\exists x)Cx$ 2, 9, Conj
   11. $(x) \sim Ax$ 3-10, IP

(4) 1. $(x)(Ax \supset Cx)$
    2. $(\exists x)Cx \supset (\exists x)(Bx \cdot Dx)$ $/(\exists x)Ax \supset (\exists x)Bx$
       3. $(\exists x)Ax$ ACP
       4. Ac 3, EI
       5. $Ac \supset Cc$ 1, UI
       6. Cc 4, 5, MP
       7. $(\exists x)Cx$ 6, EG
       8. $(\exists x)(Bx \cdot Dx)$ 2, 7, MP
       9. $Ba \cdot Da$ 8, EI
      10. Ba 9, Simp
      11. $(\exists x)Bx$ 10, EG
   12. $(\exists x)Ax \supset (\exists x)Bx$ 3-11, CP

Additional Exercises for Section 8.4

Use CP or IP in proving the following arguments valid.

(1) 1. $(\exists x)Ax \supset (x)BX$
 2. $(\exists x)Bx \supset (x)Cx$ / $(x)Ax \supset (x)Cx$

(2) 1. $(x)[(Ax \lor Bx) \supset (Cx \cdot Dx)]$ /$(x)(Ax \supset Cx)$

(3) 1. $(\exists x)Ax \supset (x)(Bx \cdot Cx)$ /$(x)(Ax \supset Cx)$

(4) 1. $(\exists x)(Ax \lor Bx) \supset (x)(Cx \cdot Dx)$
 2. $(x)(Bx \supset Dx) \supset (x)Ex$ / $(\exists x)Ex$

(5) 1. $(x)[(Bx \cdot Cx) \lor Ax]$
 2. $(x)[Bx \supset (Dx \cdot {\sim}Ex)]$
 3. $(x)(Ax \supset Fx)$ /$(x)(Ex \supset Fx)$

8.5 PROVING INVALIDITY

To show an argument invalid, it must be shown that it is possible that the premises of the argument be true and the conclusion false. Two approaches to showing arguments of predicate logic to be invalid are discussed in this section. The first is called the *counterexample method.* The second is called the *finite universe* method. Both are simply ways of showing of an invalid argument that is possible for its premises to be true and yet its conclusion false.

The counterexample method consists of inventing a substitution instance of an invalid argument form such that the substitution instance actually does have all true premises and a false conclusion.

The finite universe method for proving the invalidity of an argument in predicate logic consists in finding an interpretation of the propositions in the argument such that all the premises of the argument turn out *true* on that interpretation and the conclusion of the argument turns out *false* on that interpretation.

Interpretation of a proposition of predicate logic means designating some finite *universe of discourse,* which the proposition is then understood to be about, and then assigning a meaning in this universe for each of the predicates in the proposition. When this is done, the proposition can be explicated as meaning a certain thing about the universe, and it can be assigned a truth value. Let us proceed to see how this is done.

A universe may consist of one or more individuals. Suppose a universe consists of three named individuals *a, b,* and *c.* Then for any universally quantified proposition $(x)\mathcal{F}x$, its meaning with respect to this universe is, rather clearly, $\mathcal{F}a \cdot \mathcal{F}b \cdot \mathcal{F}c$. Moreover, any existentially quantified proposition $(\exists x)\mathcal{F}x$ has the following meaning with respect to this universe:

$$\mathcal{F}a \lor \mathcal{F}b \lor \mathcal{F}c$$

A predicate may be assigned a meaning for a universe by designating a truth value for its application to each individual in the universe. Furthermore, assigning such a meaning to all the predicates of a proposition will determine a truth value for that proposition.

Suppose, for example, that the universe has two members, *a* and *b,* and that for some predicate, for example, *P, Pa* is true and *Pb* is false. Then the statement $(x)Px$ reduces to $Pa \cdot Pb$, which is false, and the statement $(\exists x)Px$ reduces to $Pa \lor Pb$, which is true.

For any invalid argument of predicate logic, at least one universe and assignment of meaning to all the predicates will make all the premises true and the conclusion false.

Sample Exercises from Exercise 8.5. Part I

1. $(x)(Ax \supset Bx)$
   $(x)(Ax) \supset {\sim}Cx$ / $(x)(Cx \supset {\sim}Bx)$

Counterexample:

> All asps are biters.
> No asps are cobras.   /   No cobras are biters.

2. $(\exists x)(Ax \cdot Bx)$
   $(x)(Cx \supset Ax)$ / $(\exists x)(Cx \cdot Bx)$

Counterexample:

> Some animals are bears.
> All coyotes are animals.   /   Some coyotes are bears.

Sample Exercises from Exercise 8.5. Part II

(1) 1. $(x)(Ax \supset Bx)$
    2. $(x)(Ax \supset Cx)$ / $(x)(Bx \supset Cx)$

Let the universe consist of one individual a, and let Aa = F, Ba = T, and Ca = F. Then the argument has the meaning.

1. $Aa \supset Ba$
2. $Aa \supset Ca$ / $Ba \supset Ca$

As the following truth table shows, this makes all the premises true and the conclusion false:

$$Aa \supset Ba \ / \ Aa \supset Ca \ /\!/ \ Ba \supset Ca$$
$$\text{F}\boxed{\text{T}}\text{ T} \qquad \text{F}\boxed{\text{T}}\text{ F} \qquad \text{T}\boxed{\text{F}}\text{ F}$$

(2) 1. $(x)(Ax \vee Bx)$
    2. ${\sim}An$ / $(x)Bx$

Let the universe consist of two individuals n and a. (Note that n is included in the universe because it is mentioned in the argument.) Now let Aa = T, Ba = F, An = F, and Bn = T. With this universe, the argument has the meaning

1. $(Aa \vee Ba) \cdot (An \vee Bn)$
2. ${\sim}An$ / $Ba \cdot Bn$

As the following truth table shows, this makes all the premises true and the conclusion false:

$$(Aa \vee Ba) \cdot (An \vee Bn) \ / \ {\sim}An \ /\!/ \ Ba \cdot Bn$$
$$\text{T T F}\boxed{\text{T}}\text{F T T} \quad \boxed{\text{T}}\text{F} \quad \text{F}\boxed{\text{F}}\text{T}$$

Additional Exercises for Section 8.5

Prove that the following arguments are invalid by constructing a universe and a meaning assignment for the predicates that makes the premises true and the conclusion false.

(1) 1. $(\exists x)(Ax \cdot Bx)$ $/(x)Bx$

(2) 1. $(x)(Ax \supset Bx)$
    2. $(\exists x)(Ax \cdot Cx)$ $/(x)Bx$

(3) 1. $(x)[Ax \supset (Bx \cdot Cx)]$
    2. $(x)(Cx \supset Dx)$ $/(x)(Dx \supset Ax)$

(4) 1. $(x)Ax \supset (x)Bx$ $/(x)(Ax \supset Bx)$

(5) 1. $(x)(Ax \supset Bx)$ $/ (\exists x)(Ax \equiv Bx)$

8.6   RELATIONAL PREDICATES AND OVERLAPPING QUANTIFIERS

The logical apparatus of predicate logic can be extended to cover the logic of binary relations (such as *a* is a friend of *b*), ternary relations (such as *a* is between *b* and *c*), and relations of higher order. Symbolically, such relations can be expressed by a capital letter followed by lower case letters representing the items related: for example, *Fab* can be used to express that *a* is a friend of *b*, and *Babc* can be used to express that *a* is between *b* and *c*. As the latter example shows, the order of the lower case letters following the capital letter is important.

The use of variables and quantifiers with relational predicates is a natural extension of their use with nonrelational predicates. Thus, $(x)Fxa$ means that everything is a friend of *a*, and $(\exists x)Bxab$ means that something is between *a* and *b*. With relational predicates, however, there is the possibility of using variables in more than one position, and there is the possibility of multiple and overlapping quantification. Thus, we have such symbolic statements as:

$(x)(y)Fxy$, which means: for all *x* and for all *y, x* is a friend of *y*

$(x)(\exists y)Fxy$, which means: for all *x* there is some *y* such that *x* is a friend of *y*

$(\exists x)(y)Fxy$, which means: there is some *x* such that for all *y, x* is a friend of *y*

$(\exists x)(\exists y)Fxy$, which means: there is an *x* and there is a *y* such that *x* is a friend of *y*

Note that when quantifiers are mixed in type, as in the second and third of these examples, the order of quantifiers makes a crucial difference in meaning.

The apparatus of quantifiers, relational predicates (as well as non-relational predicates), and multiple, overlapping quantifiers can be combined with that of propositional logic to provide a system for translating an extensive variety of complex statements. For example, if *P* stands for the predicate of personhood and *Fxy* for the binary relation "*x* is a friend of *y*," we can perform the following translations:

Everyone has some friend: $(x)(Px \supset (\exists y)Fyx)$

Someone has everyone as a friend: $(\exists x)[Px \cdot (y)(Py \supset Fyx)]$

No one has anyone as a friend: $(x)[Px \supset (y)(Py \supset \sim Fyx)]$

Anyone who has a friend has himself as a friend: $(x)[(Px \cdot (\exists y)Fyx) \supset Fxx]$

Students often find that constructing such translations is difficult. The text provides many helpful pointers about translation, but there is simply no substitute for practice.

The rules of inference for nonrelational predicate logic apply, with only minor alteration, to the logic of relational predicates and multiple, overlapping quantifiers. One point to keep in mind in using CQ is that each quantifier of an overlapping series is understood to govern the entire string of symbols to its right. Thus, $(x)(\exists y)(z)Bxyz$ is understood to mean $(x)\{(\exists y)[(z)Bxyz]\}$. Therefore, $\sim(x)(\exists y)(z)Bxyz$ is logically equivalent to $(\exists x)\sim\{(\exists y)[(z)Bxyz]\}$, and thus to $(\exists x)(y)\sim[(z)Bxyz]$, and thus to $(\exists x)(y)(\exists z)\sim Bxyz$.

A second point to keep in mind concerns the rules for dropping and adding quantifiers: We must add an additional restriction to UG in order to prevent the possibility of deriving certain types of invalid arguments. The argument $(x)(\exists y)Pxy \; / \; (\exists y)(x)Pxy$ is clearly invalid. (To see this, consider Pxy to mean that x is a number greater than the number y; then the premise says that for every number there is a greater one, and the conclusion says that there is a greatest number; clearly this inference is wrong.) Without some restriction on UG, we could carry out the following derivation:

1. $(x)(\exists y)Pxy$
2. $(\exists y)Pxy$ 1, UI
3. Pxc 2, EI
4. $(x)Pxc$ 3, UG (invalid)
5. $(\exists y)(x)Pxy$ 4, EG

The basic reason step 4 is invalid is that the "choice" of c in line 3 is dependent on x's already having been specified, whereas in line 4 it is made to appear as if c is independent of the specification of x. The prevent such inferences as line 4, then, we need the following restriction on UN: UG must not be used if the line being generalized upon by UG contains a constant obtained from EI (a so-called existential name) and if the variable being generalized upon is ungoverned by a quantifier in the line where that constant was introduced by the EI step. Let us attempt to phrase this restriction on UG a bit more clearly. UG has the following form:

$$\text{UG} \quad \frac{Fy}{(x)Fx}$$

The restriction is as follows: UG must not be applied to the line Fy if Fy contains a constant, say c, such that this constant c has been introduced by an EI step at some line in the proof in which line the variable y occurs ungoverned by any quantifier.

Conditional and indirect proof are used the same way with relational predicates as with nonrelational predicates; the crucial point to keep in mind is the restriction on UG that must be observed inside the scope of assumptions. That is to say, inside the scope of any assumption, UG must not be applied to the line Fy if the variable y occurs in that assumption ungoverned by any quantifier. (In understanding this restriction, keep in mind that by "the assumption" is meant merely the first line of the scope: every assumption is the first line of its own scope.)

A final point of caution must be mentioned with regard to universal instantiation: When a variable is introduced by UI into a proof, this variable must not be identical to the variable of a quantifier within whose governance its introduced occurrence falls. The following bogus "proof" illustrates an incorrect use of UI:

1. $(x)(\exists y)Pxy$
2. $(\exists y)Pyy$ 1, UI (invalid)

If the variable introduced into line 2 were not y but some other variable, say x, or z, the instantiation would be correct.

It is important that in using UG or EG the quantifiers capture only the variables they are intended to capture. They should not capture variables that are already bound by other quantifiers, and they should not capture other variables that are ungoverned by any quantifiers in the statement function. These qualifications rule out such invalid inferences as:

1. $(\exists x)Pxy$
2. $(x)(\exists x)Pxx$ 1, UG (invalid)

Care should also be taken to avoid inferences such as:

1. $(\exists x)Pxc$
2. $(\exists x)(\exists x)Pxx$ 1, EG (invalid)

and

1. $(x)(\exists y)(Fx \equiv \sim Fy)$
2. $(\exists x)(Fx \equiv \sim Fy)$ 1, UI
3. $Fx \equiv \sim Fc$ 2, EI
4. $(\exists x)(Fx \equiv \sim Fx)$ 3, EG (invalid)

Sample Exercises from Exercise 8.6. Part I

1. Charmaine read *Paradise Lost.*

   Rcp

2. Whoever reads *Paradise Lost* is educated.

   $(x)[(Px \cdot Rxp) \supset Ex]$ Note: $Px = x$ is a person

3. James is a friend of either Ellen or Connie.

   Fje ∨ *Fjc*

4. If James has any friends, then Marlene is one of them.

   $(\exists x)Fxj \supset Fmj$

   A second correct answer—correct because it is logically equivalent to the first answer—is

   $(x)(Fxj \supset Fmj)$

   It is to be noted that neither of these correct answers is equivalent to

   $(x)Fxj \supset Fmj$

   which translates "If *everything* is a friend of James, then Marlene is a friend of James."

Sample Exercises from Exercise 8.6. Part II

(1) 1. $(x)[Ax \supset (y)Bxy]$
     2. Am / $(y)Bmy$
     3. $Am \supset (y)Bmy$ 1, UI
     4. $(y)Bmy$ 2, 3, MP

(2) 1. $(x)[Ax \supset (y)(By \supset Cxy)]$
     2. $Am \cdot Bn$ / Cmn
     3. $Am \supset (y)(By \supset Cmy)$ 1, UI
     4. Am 2, Simp
     5. $(y)(By \supset Cmy)$ 3, 4, MP
     6. $Bn \cdot Am$ 2, Com

7.	Bn	6, Simp
8.	$Bn \supset Cmn$	5, UI
9.	Cmn	7, 8, MP

(3)	1.	$(\exists x)[Ax \cdot (y)(By \supset Cxy)]$	
	2.	$(\exists x)Ax \supset Bj$	$/ (\exists x)Cxj$
	3.	$Ac \cdot (y)(By \supset Ccy)$	1, EI
	4.	Ac	3, Simp
	5.	$(\exists x)Ax$	4, EG
	6.	Bj	2, 5, MP
	7.	$(y)(By \supset Ccy) \cdot Ac$	3, Com
	8.	$(y)(By \supset Ccy)$	7, Simp
	9.	$Bj \supset Ccj$	8, UI
	10.	Ccj	6, 9, MP
	11.	$(\exists x)Cxj$	10, EG

(4)	1.	$(x)(\exists y)(Ax \supset By)$	$/ (x)Ax \supset (\exists y)By$
	2.	$(x)Ax$	ACP
	3.	$(\exists y)(Ax \supset By)$	1, UI
	4.	$Ax \supset Bc$	3, EI
	5.	Ax	2, UI
	6.	Bc	4, 5, MP
	7.	$(\exists y)By$	6, EG
	8.	$(x)Ax \supset (\exists y)By$	2-7, CP

Additional Exercises for Section 8.6

I. Translate the following statements into symbolic propositions, using the following predicates and relations: $Px = x$ is a person; $Txy = x$ is taller than y; $LXY = x$ likes y.

1. No one is taller than John.

2. No one is taller than himself.

3. Everyone likes somebody.

4. No one likes everybody.

5. No one is liked by everybody.

6. Everyone likes at least one person who is taller than she.

7. There is somebody who likes anyone who is taller than he.

8. No one likes anyone who is not taller than she.

9. Everyone does not like at least one person who is taller than he.

10. If everyone likes anybody who is not taller than she, then everyone likes herself.

II. Prove the following symbolized arguments valid.

(1)	1.	$(x)(\exists y)Fxy \supset (x)Gxx$	
	2.	$(\exists y)(x)Fxy$	$/ (x)Gxx$

(2) 1. $(x)(y)Fxy$ $/ (\exists z) Fzz$

(3) 1. $(x)(y)(Fxy \cdot Gyx)$ $/ (z)(Fzz \cdot Gzz)$

(4) 1. $(x)[Fx \supset (y)Gy]$ $/ (\exists x)Fx \supset (\exists y)Gy$

(5) 1. $(x)Fx \cdot (y)Gy$ $/ (x)(y)(Fx \cdot Gy)$

(6) 1. $(x)(\exists y)Ixy$
     2. $(x)(y)(Ixy \supset \sim Mxy)$ $/ (x)(\exists y)\sim Mxy$

(7) 1. $(x)(y)(z)[Bxyz \supset (Lx \cdot Lyz)]$
     2. $(x)(y)(Lxy \supset \sim Ixy) / (x)(y)(z)[Bxyz \supset \sim(Ixy \lor Iyz)]$

(8) 1. $(x)(y)(z)[Bxyz \supset (Lxy \cdot Lyz)]$
     2. $(x)Ixx$
     3. $(x)(y)(Ixy \supset \sim Lxy)$ $/ (x)(y) \sim Bxxy$

(9) 1. $(x)(y)(Lxy \lor Lyx)$
     2. $(x)(y)[(Lxy \cdot Lyx) \supset Ixy]$ $/ (x)(y)[\sim Ixy \supset (Lxy \equiv \sim Lyx)]$

(10) 1. $(x)(y)(z)[(Lxy \cdot Lyz) \supset Lxz]$
     2. $(x)(y)(Lxy \supset Lyx)$ $/ (x)[(\exists y)Lxy \supset Lxx]$

8.7 IDENTITY

Identity is a binary relation (that is, a relation with two relata) that has such special qualities that additional rules of inference must be introduced in order adequately to formalize the meaning of this relation.

When we say that a named individual a is identical to (or: with) a named individual b, we are saying that a and b are *one and the same individual*. In symbolizing the relation of identity, a special symbol is used, namely the mathematician's equal sign "=". Thus to say that a is identical with b we write

$$a = b \qquad .$$

By way of abbreviation, for

$$\sim(a = b)$$

we may write

$$a \neq b \qquad .$$

Identity is a relation that is not merely of paramount importance in mathematics but also extremely useful in translating into logical symbols many of the things we say in everyday life. For example, identity—as the following paradigms illustrate—may be used to translate "Only a F's," "The only F is a," "No F except a is G," "All F's except a are G," and statements that are variants of these.

"Only a F's (is an F)"

is translated as

$$Fa \cdot (x) (Fx \supset x = a)$$

"The only F is a"

is translated as

$$Fa \cdot (x)\,(Fx \supset x = a) \qquad .$$

"No F except a is G"

is translated as

$$Fa \cdot Ga \cdot (x)\,[(Fx \cdot Gx) \supset x = a] \qquad .$$

"All F's except a are G"

is translated as

$$Fa \cdot {\sim}Ga \cdot (x)\,[(Fx \cdot x \neq a) \supset Gx] \qquad .$$

Identity may also be used with binary relations that are understood to denote orderings (such as: greater than, less than, bigger than, taller than, etc.) to express judgments of maximality. For example, if

$$Bxy$$

stands for "x is bigger than y," then to express that there is a biggest thing, we write

$$(\exists x)(y)(x \neq y \supset Bxy)$$

To express that Paul Bunyan is the biggest lumberjack, we would write (letting b stand for Paul Bunyan and Lx stand for "x is a lumberjack"):

$$Lb \cdot (x)\,[(Lx \cdot x \neq b) \supset Bbx]$$

By using identity, we may also express statements asserting that there are *at most* a given number of items (of some sort), statements asserting that there are *at least* a given number of items (of some sort), and (by conjoining these two) statements asserting that there are *exactly* a given number of items (of some sort). The following examples show how to do this.

"There is at most one F"

is translated as

$$(x)\,(y)\,[(Fx \cdot Fy) \supset x = y]$$

"There are at most two F's"

is translated as $(x)\,(y)\,(z)\,[(Fx \cdot Fy \cdot Fz) \supset (x = y \lor x = z \lor y = z)]$.

The general pattern should be clear.

"There is at least one F"

is translated as

$$(\exists x)Fx$$

"There are at least two F's"

is translated as

$$(\exists x)\,(\exists y)\,(Fx \cdot Fy \cdot x \neq y)$$

The general pattern should be clear.

To say that there is exactly a given number of items (of some sort) we simply conjoin the statement that there are at most this number of (such) items with the statement that there are at least this number of (such) items. Thus

"There is exactly one F"

is translated as

$$(x)\,(y)\,[(Fx \cdot Fy) \supset x = y] \cdot (\exists x)Fx$$

This assertion is logically equivalent to, and thus also expressible as:

$$(\exists x)[Fx \cdot (y)\,(Fy \supset x = y)]$$

In a fashion similar to the one just employed, other "there are exactly" statements may be expressed by simply conjoining a "there are at most" statement with a "there are at least" statement. Also, such conjunctions can always be expressed in a logically equivalent statement that is a bit simpler than the conjunction. (The Hurley text uses this latter method.)

In order to employ identity in constructing deductions, we need some special inferential forms. A minimal collection of such inferential forms would rely merely on two facts about identity: first, that everything is identical with itself, namely that

$$(x)x = x \qquad ,$$

and that if something is identical with something else, then whatever is true of that something is also true of that something else. All rules of inference using identity can be derived from these two facts. In order to have a fairly serviceable system for constructing deductions using identity, however, we introduce a system involving three rules of inference, all three called

$$\text{Id} \qquad .$$

In understanding these rules, we must first understand that both a and b are to be understood as designating any individual variable or any individual constant.

Rules for Using Identity: (ID)

(1) $a = a$ (2) $a = b :: b = a$ (3) $\mathscr{F}a$

$$\dfrac{a = b}{\mathscr{F}b}$$

The first Id rule simply allows us to introduce a line into a proof. The second ID rule allows us to substitute any identity statement with a corresponding identity statement in which the left and right entries have been reversed. The third rule is a formal way of saying that if something (a) is identical with something else (b), then whatever is true of that something ($\mathscr{F}$) is also true of that something else. To apply the third Id rule, b is substituted for one or more occurrence of a. Since special restrictions apply if a is a variable that is quantified over, it is initially best for students to apply the third Id rule only where a and b are constants.

Sample Exercises from Exercise 8.7. Part II

(2) Ronald Reagan was the oldest U.S. President. Woodrow Wilson was a U.S. President. Woodrow Wilson is not Ronald Reagan. Therefore, Ronald Reagan was older than Woodrow Wilson.

1. $Ur \cdot (x) [(Ux \cdot x \neq r) \supset Orx]$

2. Uw

3. $w \neq r$ / Orw

4. Ur 1, Simp

5. $(x)[(Ux \cdot x \neq r) \supset Orx]$ 1, Com, Simp

6. $(Uw \cdot w \neq r) \supset Orw$ 5, UI

7. $Uw \cdot w \neq r$ 2, 3, Conj

8. Orw 6, 7, MP

(3) The artist who painted the Mona Lisa was a Florentine. Leonardo is the artist who painted the Mona Lisa. Therefore, Leonardo was a Florentine.

1. $(\exists x)\{Ax \cdot Pxm \cdot (y)[(Ay \cdot Pym) \supset x = y] \cdot Fx\}$

2. $(\exists x)\{Ax \cdot Pxm \cdot (y)[(Ay \cdot Pym) \supset x = y] \cdot l = x\}$ / Fl

3. $Aa \cdot Pam \cdot (y)[(Ay \cdot Pym) \supset a = y] \cdot Fa$ 1, EI

4. $Aa \cdot Pam$ 3, Simp

5. $(y)[(Ay \cdot Pym) \supset a = y]$ 3, Com, Assoc, Simp

6. Fa 3, Com, Simp

7. $Ab \cdot Pbm \cdot (y)[(Ay \cdot Pym) \supset b = y] \cdot l = b$ 2, EI

8. $Ab \cdot Pbm$ 7, Simp

9. $l = b$ 7, Com, Simp

10. $(Ab \cdot Pbm) \supset a = b$ 5, UI

11. $a = b$ 8, 10, MP

12. $b = a$ 11, Id

13. $l = a$ 9, 12, Id

14. $a = l$ 13, Id

15. Fl 6, 14, Id

Additional Exercises for Section 8.7

(1) 1. $a = b$
     2. $b = c$ / $c = a$

(2) 1. Fa / $(\exists x)(Fx \cdot x = a)$

(3) 1. $(x)(\exists y)(x = y) \supset Fa$ / Fa

(4) 1. $(x)(y)[(Fx \cdot Fy) \supset x = y] \cdot (\exists x)Fx$ / $(\exists x)[Fx \cdot (y)(Fy \supset x = y)]$

(5) 1. $(\exists x)[Fx \cdot (y)(Fy \supset x = y)]$ / $(x)(y)[(Fx \cdot Fy) \supset x = y] \cdot (\exists x)Fx$

9
INDUCTION

9.1 ANALOGY AND LEGAL AND MORAL REASONING

Analogical reasoning is among the most important forms of inductive reasoning used in everyday life; it is also one of the most typical forms of reasoning used in legal and moral contexts. Analogical reasoning has already been discussed in Chapter 3, Section 3, where the informal fallacy of *weak analogy* was presented. In this first section of Chapter 9 this form of inductive reasoning will be discussed in somewhat greater detail.

Most generally, an analogical inference has the following form:

A_1 has characteristics $c_1, c_2, \ldots, c_n$, and characteristic z.
A_2 has characteristics $c_1, c_2, \ldots, c_n$, and characteristic z.
.

.

.

A_k has characteristics $c_1, c_2, \ldots, c_n$, and characteristic z.
B has characteristics $c_1, c_2, \ldots, c_n$.

Therefore, B has characteristic z (or: probably has characteristic z).

In this scheme, the A_i and B might be things, facts, situations, events, conditions, etc. The A_i are called the *primary analogates* of the argument from analogy; B is called the *secondary analogate* of the argument. The characteristics $c_1, c_2, \ldots, c_n$ are called the *similarities* between the primary analogates on the one hand and the secondary analogate on the other hand. The number k is the primary analogates, and the number n is the number of the similarities.

The strength of an argument from analogy depends on a number of factors, of which six will be discussed here.

Factor 1: The relevance of the similarities to the characteristic z. If there is some important relation of relevance between the similarities $c_1, c_2, \ldots, c_n$ and the characteristic z, then (other factors being ignored) the argument tends to be a strong one. A typical "important relation of relevance" would be, for example, a causal connection or an invariable association between the similarities and z. In legal and moral contexts as "important relation of relevance" would be that the similarities conjointly define z or at least imply z in the absence of any defeating legal or moral considerations.

Factor 2: The number n of the similarities. The larger n is, the greater the strength of the argument (other factors being ignored).

Factor 3: The nature and degree of disanalogies between the primary analogates A_i and the secondary analogate B. A *disanalogy* (or dissimilarity) between the A_i and B is a characteristic x that (most of) the A_i have but that B does not have or alternatively that (most of) the A_i do not have but that B does have. If the disanalogies between the A_i and the B are relevant to the having or not having of characteristic z, and if the disanalogies are sufficiently numerous, then the argument is ordinarily weakened (other factors being ignored).

Factor 4: The number k of primary analogates. The larger k is, the greater the strength of the argument (other factors being ignored).

Factor 5: Diversity among the primary analogates A_i. The greater the diversity of the primary analogates, the greater the strength of the argument (other factors being ignored).

Factor 6: The specificity of the characteristic z. The more specifically and precisely defined z is, the weaker the argument (other factors being ignored).

Sample Exercise from Exercise 9.1. Part II

2. Harold needs to have his rugs cleaned, and his friend Veronica reports that Ajax Carpet Service did an excellent job on her rugs. From this, Harold concludes that Ajax will do an equally good job on his rugs. How do the following facts bear on Harold's argument?

    a. Veronica hired Ajax several times, and Ajax always did an excellent job.
    b. Veronica's rugs are wool, whereas Harold's are nylon.
    c. Veronica's carpets never had any stains on them before they were cleaned, but Harold's have several large stains.
    d. Veronica always had her rugs cleaned in mid-October, whereas Harold wants his done just a week before Easter.
    e. Harold knows of six additional people who have had their carpets cleaned by Ajax, and all six have been very pleased.
    f. All six own rugs made of different material.
    g. All six were born in Massachusetts.
    h. Ajax has recently undergone a change in management.
    i. The Environmental Protection Agency recently banned the cleaning solution Ajax has used for many years.
    j. Harold changes his conclusion to state that Ajax will get his carpets approximately as clean as it has gotten Veronica's.

    a. This fact strengthens the argument by increasing the number of primary analogates.
    b. This fact weakens the argument by being a point of disanalogy between the primary analogate and the secondary analogate.
    c. This fact weakens the argument by being a point of disanalogy between the primary analogate and the secondary analogate.
    d. This is a point of disanalogy between the primary analogate and the secondary analogate. It is, however, not a particularly important or relevant point of disanalogy because there is no obvious connection between success in cleaning carpets and the time of year that carpet cleaning is done. (If some connection of this sort has been established previously, then the point of disanalogy might be considered more important than one would typically find it to be.) Thus the argument is weakened, but weakened only very slightly, indeed.
    e. This fact strengthens the argument by increasing the number of primary analogates.
    f. This fact strengthens the argument by establishing considerable diversity among the primary analogates.
    g. This fact would not seem to be a relevant consideration in evaluating the argument: there would not seem to be any connection between being born in Massachusetts and successfully having one's carpet cleaned.
    h. This fact weakens the argument by being a point of disanalogy between the primary analogate and the secondary analogate.
    i. This fact weakens the argument by being a point of disanalogy between the primary analogate and the secondary analogate.
    j. This fact strengthens the argument by making the characteristic (or the conclusion) vaguer, less specific.

9.2 CAUSALITY AND MILL'S METHODS

The notion of causation is to some extent ambiguous. When we say that A is the cause of *B* or a cause of *B*, we can mean that *A* is a necessary condition of *B*, that *A* is a sufficient condition of *B*, or that *A* is both a necessary and sufficient condition of *B*. There are deep philosophical difficulties concerning the relation between asserting causal connections among particular events and asserting general causal statements about types of events. These difficulties will be largely ignored here. When events *A* and *B* are spoken of, it will usually be clear when *particular* events are being discussed and when *types* of events are being discussed.

When cause as necessary condition and cause as sufficient condition are distinguished, Mill's methods of identifying causes can be broken down into a more refined classification that Mill himself presented. The more refined classification is presented here.

The *direct method of agreement* is a method for identifying a cause in the sense of a necessary condition. To use it, examine all cases in which a given effect *E* is presented and try to find some factor *F* that is present in all these cases. That is to say, eliminate any factor that is not present in all of the cases. Any factor *F* that remains is a candidate for a necessary condition of *E* and consequently may be a cause of *E* in this sense.

The *inverse method of agreement* is a method for identifying a cause in the sense of a sufficient condition. To use it, examine all cases in which a given effect *E* is absent and try to find some factor *F* that is also absent. Eliminate any factor that is present whenever *E* is absent. Any factor that remains will be such that its nonpresence may be a necessary condition of the nonpresence of *E*. In other words, then, the presence of this factor may be a sufficient condition for the presence of *E* and consequently may be a cause of *E* in this sense.

The *double method of agreement* is simply a combination of the direct method of agreement and the inverse method of agreement. To use it, examine all cases in which a given effect *E* is present and all cases in which it is absent. Try to find a factor *F* that is present when *E* is present and absent when *E* is absent. This factor, if it exists, may be a necessary and sufficient condition for *E* and thus may be a cause of it in this sense.

The *method of difference* consists in examining two cases (or classes of cases), one of which exhibits an effect *E* and the other of which does not. To use it, try to find a single factor *F* that is present in the case(s) in which *E* is present and absent in the case(s) in which *E* is absent. The factor *F* is a candidate for what differentiates the two cases (or classes of cases). It is then a candidate for a cause in the sense of a sufficient condition.

The *joint method of agreement and difference* consists in combining the direct method of agreement with the method of difference. The result is a candidate for a cause in the sense of a necessary and sufficient condition.

The *method of residues* consists in "subtracting" known and causal connections from other, more complex, known causal relations, leaving as a candidate for a causal connection the remaining relation. If there is a causal connection between a complex or conjunctive event *A* and another such event *B*, and if event *a* is an isolatable part or conjunct of event *A*, and *b* is an isolatable part or conjunct of event *B*, and if there is a known causal relation between *a* and *b*, then it can be concluded that there is a probable causal connection between the residue *A* − *a* and the residue *B* − *b*. (The nature of the subtraction here is, of course, somewhat unclear.)

The *method of concomitant variation* consists in identifying a functional relation (perhaps expressible as an equation) between a factor *F* that admits of quantity or degree and a factor *E* that admits of quantity or degree, such that variations in the quantity of *F* correspond with variations in the quantity of *E*. This functional relation may be direct or inverse. When such a relation is round, it may be concluded that *F* and *E* are probably causally related.

1. Throwing a brick through a window will cause the window to break.

    This is a statement of a *sufficient* condition for the window to break. Obviously, throwing a brick is not necessary for the window to break.

2. Heating an iron rod causes it to expand.

    This is a statement of sufficient condition for the iron rod to expand. Under normal conditions it is also necessary, but in general it is not a necessary condition: an iron rod will expand under certain sorts of magnetic fields, when great pressure is taken off it, and so forth.

Additional Exercises for Section 9.2

Identify the Mill's method that is being employed in each of the following inferences.

1. Virus *V* was found in every case of sinusitis that we examined. We conclude, then, that virus *V* is a cause of sinusitis.

2. We have never found a disturbed home life in the background of any of our students who do not have trouble in school. We may conclude, then, that a disturbed home life is a cause of student trouble in school.

3. We compared two classes of rats, one with stunted growth and one without stunted growth. The stunted rats had an unusual amount of calcium in their early diets, whereas the nonstunted rats had early diets with a normal amount of calcium. We concluded that abnormal amounts of calcium in the early diet of rats is a cause of stunting in their growth.

4. We notice that a rise in elevation is correlated with a fall in the level of mercury in a barometer. We conclude that the elevation above sea level determines the height of mercury in a barometer.

5. Plants with root rot are always found to be heavily watered. We have never seen a plant without root rot that was heavily watered. It can be concluded, then, that heavy watering of plants causes them to have root rot.

9.3 PROBABILITY

The notion of probability, like that of causality, is crucial for the study of induction. But like causality, probability can have different meanings. For example, if we refer to the probability of drawing a spade from a standard deck of cards, we have in mind the mathematical procedure of comparing the thirteen spades in a standard deck to the fifty-two cards; but if we refer to the probability that a meteor of gigantic size collided with the earth millions of years ago, we have in mind something very different from such a mathematical procedure.

Different meanings of probability can be correlated with different theories or interpretations of probability. There are, for example, the classical theory, the relative-frequency theory, and the subjectivist theory of probability, each of which is discussed in the text. These theories of probability have in common what is known as the *probability calculus*. The probability calculus is a set of mathematical formulas for computing probabilities. It is usually represented by a set of axioms and the theorems that follow logically from these axioms. But the content of the probability calculus is perhaps best explained in conjunction with an account of the classical theory.

The *classical theory* begins with the idea of an experiment that can have n discrete possible outcomes. According the prin*ciple of indifference*, each outcome is equally likely; in other words, the n outcomes are equiprobable. Moreover, the outcomes of an experiment can classified into types. Then, the probability that the result of the experiment will be an outcome of type A is defined by the formula

$$P(A) = f/n,$$

where f is the number of outcomes of type A. For example, the probability of drawing a spade from a standard deck is $13/52 = 1/4$, since there are 52 equiprobable outcomes, 13 of which are spades.

Since outcomes are of various types, we may consider the outcomes of logically combining given types. For example, we may consider the probability that the result of an experiment is *not* of type A, the probability that the result is both of type A and of type B, and so forth. The probability calculus enables us to compute such probabilities. For example, the probability that a result is not of type A is computed by the *negation rule* to be

$$P(\text{not-}A) = (n - f)/n = 1 - f/n = 1 - P(A)$$

Clearly, the probability of a result of a type that *necessarily* results, such as "A or not-A," is 1; and the probability of a result of a type that cannot happen, such as "A and not-A," is 0.

Computing probabilities of conjunctive types is a bit more complicated. When two types are *independent* of each other (that is, when an occurrence of the one type has no influence one way or the other on the probability of an occurrence of the other type), the *restricted conjunction rule* may be used to compute the probability of the conjunction of the two types:

$$P(A \text{ and } B) = P(A) \times P(B)$$

Alternatively, the restricted conjunction rule may be used as a definition of the independence of two event types.

When two event types are not independent of each other, we must use the *general conjunction rule*. This rule involves an expression that quantifies the degree of influence that one event type has on the other: $P(B \text{ given } A)$. The meaning of this term is "the probability that B occurs *given that* A occurs (or has occurred)." The general conjunction rule, then, is

$$P(A \text{ and } B) = P(A) \times P(B \text{ given } A)$$

When two event types are mutually exclusive, the probability that the result of an experiment is one or the other of these types, written $P(A \text{ or } B)$, is given by the *restricted disjunction rule*:

$$P(A \text{ or } B) = P(A) + P(B)$$

When two event types are not mutually exclusive, the probability that the result of the experiment is one or the other (or both) of these types is given by the *general disjunction rule*:

$$P(A \text{ or } B) = P(A) + P(B) - P(A \text{ and } B)$$

In order to relate the two conditional probabilities $P(A \text{ given } B)$ and $P(B \text{ given } A)$ to each other, there is a useful formula known as *Bayes's Theorem*. It may be derived from the foregoing considerations as follows.

First, by the general conjunction rule, applied twice, we have that

$$P(A \text{ and } B) = P(B \text{ given } A) \times P(A)$$

and

$$P(B \text{ and } A) = P(A \text{ given } B) \times P(B).$$

Clearly, however, by the commutivity of conjunction, $P(A \text{ and } B) = P(B \text{ and } A)$, so that, by setting equals equal, we have that

$$P(A \text{ given } B) \times P(B) = P(B \text{ given } A) \times P(A).$$

By dividing both sides of this equation by $P(B)$ we obtain

$$P(A \text{ given } B) = \frac{P(B \text{ given } A) \times P(A)}{P(B)}.$$

But, by the restricted disjunction rule,

$$P(B) = P(B \text{ and } A) + P(B \text{ and not-}A).$$

It follows by substitution that

$$P(A \text{ given } B) = \frac{P(B \text{ given } A) \times P(A)}{P(B \text{ and } A) + P(B \text{ and not-}A)}.$$

Now, as we have previously seen, $P(B \text{ and } A) = P(B \text{ given } A) \times P(A)$. Similarly, we have that $P(B \text{ and not-}A) = P(B \text{ given not-}A) \times P(\text{not-}A)$. Hence, by substituting into the denominator of the equation given just above for $P(A \text{ given } B)$, we obtain the result that

$$P(A \text{ given } B) = \frac{P(B \text{ given } A) \times P(A)}{[P(B \text{ given } A) \times P(A)] + [P(B \text{ given not-}A) \times P(\text{not-}A)]}.$$

This result is Bayes's Theorem.

The above rules for calculating probabilities constitute the core of the probability calculus. The same calculus can also be associated with theories of probability other than the classical theory, although the association is more complicated to explain, and will be omitted here in favor of a brief exposition of the basic ideas of the relative-frequency theory and the subjectivist theory.

With the *relative-frequency theory*, an experiment of a given type, and that has various outcomes of given types, is performed repeatedly, while observations are made of the type of outcome resulting from each performance of the experiment. After n_o such performances, f_o outcomes of type A are observed. The probability of an outcome of type A is then computed as

$$P(A) = n_o / f_o$$

Clearly, $P(A)$ may be computed differently, depending on the number of performances of the experiment. But typically as n_o gets larger and larger, $P(A)$ begins to settle about some fixed value; that is, $P(A)$ differs from this fixed value by smaller and smaller amounts. We may say, then, that the probability of A is this fixed, limiting value of the relative frequency n_o / f_o as n_o increases indefinitely.

According to the *subjectivist theory* of probability, a probability number (that is, a number between zero and one) is assigned to various types of outcomes of a given type of experiment. The assignment is made by some person on the basis of his or her subjective expectation of the likelihood that an outcome of a given type will occur. The main point of subjectivist theory is that if the subjective assignments are not made consistently with the probability calculus, then those assignments are irrational in the following sense: a bet or wager may be made with the

124

person, which he or she is bound to lose. Subjectivist probability theory is helpful in analyzing assignments of probability to one-of-a-kind situations.

Sample Exercises from Exercise 9.3. Part I

1. The probability of rolling a five on a single die is 1/6. There is one way to roll a five out of six possible outcomes.

2. If 273 Ajax trucks out of a possible 9,750 developed transmission problems within the first two years of operation, then the probability that an Ajax truck will develop transmission problems within the first two years is 273/9,750.

Additional Exercises for Section 9.3

Compute the following probabilities.

1. The probability of not drawing a king in a draw from a standard deck of cards.

2. The probability of drawing both a king and a spade.

3. The probability of drawing a king or a spade or both.

4. The probability of drawing a king given that a spade is drawn.

5. The probability of not drawing a king given that a spade is not drawn.

6. The probability of drawing a face card.

7. The probability of rolling a total of seven on a single roll of a pair of standard dice.

8. The probability of rolling a total of either two or twelve.

9. The probability of throwing a roll such that one or the other of the dice shows a six, given that a total of seven is thrown.

10. The probability of neither die showing a four given that a total of six is rolled.

9.4   STATISTICAL REASONING

Many difficulties exist with regard to statistical reasoning. Five areas of difficulty are identified and discussed in the text.

1. *Samples.* Generalizations based on samples should be made only when the sample is randomly selected and large enough. In addition, attributing characteristics to members of a sample should be free of bias on the part of the persons attributing those characteristics.

2. *The Meaning of Average.* The word "average" may mean various things:

   a. The *mean*—the sum of the individual values of the data divided by the number of data in the set.
   b. The *median*—the midpoint of the data values when they are arranged in a linear order according to value.
   c. The *mode*—the particular data value occurring with the greatest frequency.

Confusing these very different averages can result in misguided conclusions, as the text shows.

3. *Dispersion.* This term refers to how widely spaced or spread out the values of the data are. Ignoring dispersion in statistical descriptions of data can lead to mistaken conclusions, as the text shows.

Three measures of dispersion are commonly used. The *range* of a set of data is the difference between the largest and the smallest data value. The *variance* of a set of data and the *standard deviation* of a set of data both measure the extent to which the data deviate from the mean value. There is an older way and a newer way to compute these values. The older way is a bit simpler, so it is the one given here. To compute the variance of a set of data values, find the difference between each data value in the set and the *mean* of the set, then square each of these differences (that is, multiply the difference by itself). Then, the mean of these squared differences is the variance. To find the standard deviation, simply take the square root of the variance. (The definitions of the new-style variance and standard deviation may be found in any book on statistics.)

4. *Graphs and Pictograms.* Such representations can mislead, as the text shows, because of suggestive scaling of graph axes, because of the omission (or chopping off) of portions of the axes, or because of incorrectly proportioned illustrations.

5. *Percentages.* Percentages, for example percentage differences, should always be given with a clear *base* of comparison. If this is not done, the meaning of the percentage is undeterminable.

Sample Exercises from Exercise 9.4. Part I

1. To test the algae content in a lake, a biologist took a sample of the water at one end. The algae in the sample registered 5 micrograms per liter. Therefore, the algae in the lake at that time registered 5 micrograms per liter.

   The conclusion is based on a sample that is not likely to be representative.

2. To estimate public support for a new municipality-funded convention center, researchers surveyed 100 homeowners in one of the city's fashionable neighborhoods. They found that 89 percent of those sampled were enthusiastic about the project. Therefore, we may conclude that 89 percent of the city's residents favor the convention center.

   The conclusion is based on a nonrepresentative sample.

Additional Exercises for Section 9.4

Identify the area of statistical difficulty that casts doubt on the following statistical reasonings:

1. Brand X acne medicine is 76 percent better than its best competitor. Thus, you should buy Brand X.

2. Of the ministers surveyed, 80 percent said they would vote Republican in the election. So the Republicans will win overwhelmingly.

3. The average income—mean, median, and mode—in this neighborhood is $50,000 per year. We may conclude that most of the people in it are solidly middle class.

4. When slave owners asked slaves if they wanted to be free, an overwhelming number of them said they preferred to remain slaves. Clearly, then, freeing the slaves was something that took place against their will.

5. The average age of the students in this class is 19.6 years. So there must be at least several students in this class between 19 and 20 years of age.

9.5   HYPOTHETICAL REASONING

Hypothetical reasoning is inferring from a set of data to a hypothesis that explains these data. Once a hypothesis has been formulated, it may be tested against the data it is supposed to explain. It also may be tested by using it to predict new data and then seeing whether the prediction is correct.

For a hypothesis to be acceptable, it must at least be internally consistent and coherent. *Coherent* means that the hypothesis must be so constituted internally that its basic concepts and assertions do not raise insuperable problems, or more problems than the hypothesis was invented to solve. Also, a hypothesis must be adequate. That is, it must be able to explain the data that it was invented to explain.

The most elementary form of hypothetical reasoning is generalization. But historically, the most interesting and fruitful hypotheses, both in the sciences and in philosophy, have involved great intuitive, creative leaps of imagination. Obviously, then, the logic of hypothesis construction—if there is such a logic—is a matter of great complexity. As a matter of fact, this whole topic is a matter of spirited controversy. Much about hypothetical reasoning can be learned simply by studying the history of the sciences and of philosophy.

ANSWERS TO ADDITIONAL EXERCISES

1.1

1. P: Cigarette smoking is a leading cause of cancer.
   C: Only a fool or a daredevil smokes cigarettes.

2. P_1: If we had world enough and time, this coyness would not be a crime
   P_2: We don't have world enough and time.
   C: This coyness is a crime.

3. P: The square root of the number two is an irrational number.
   C: The hypotenuse of an isosceles right triangle is not commensurable with its side.

4. P_1: No man is an island.
   P_2: Every man is a piece of the continent.
   P_3: Every man is a part of the main.
   C: No one should send to know for whom the bell tolls.

5. P_1: Without the freedom to buy and sell, the freedom to speak is absent.
   P_2: In the absence of a free market, tyranny flourishes.
   C: A free market is necessary for a free society.

6. P_1: He jests at scars that never felt a wound.
   P_2: Mercutio jests at scars.
   C: Mercutio never felt a wound.

7. P_1: It takes years and years for adult Americans to learn to speak the French language well.
   P_2: In France even little children speak the French language well.
   C: The French are the most intelligent people in the world.

8. P_1: If the world has not existed from eternity, then at some time there was nothing at all.
   P_2: Out of nothing at all nothing at all could come.
   C: The world has existed from eternity.

9. P_1: The world must have existed from eternity.
   P_2: Eternity includes 6006 B.C.
   C: The world must have existed in 6006 B.C.

10. P_1: There are many average families in the United States.
    P_2: The average U.S. family has 2.2 children.
    P_3: Two-tenths of a child is a part of a child.
    C: Many U.S. families have parts of children in them.

1. This is not an argument but rather an explanation of why the beaker exploded.

2. This is an argument with the conclusion that it is undoubtable that there are flying saucers.

3. This is an argument with the conclusion that John probably ate something that did not agree with him.

4. This is not an argument. Rather it is an explanation of why John stayed home from the dance.

5. This is not an argument but rather a conditional statement.

6. This is not an argument but rather a conditional statement.

7. This is not an argument but rather an illustration.

8. This is an argument with the conclusion that the world is in much greater danger of a nuclear confrontation than one might at first think.

9. This is not an argument but rather a string of statements that amount more or less to a description.

10. This is an argument with the conclusion that a government cannot be considered responsible if it does not deal with the problem of inflation.

1.3

1. Inductive argument: an inductive generalization.

2. Deductive argument.

3. Inductive argument: an argument based on signs.

4. Inductive argument from effect to cause.

5. Inductive argument: an argument from analogy.

6. Inductive argument: a prediction.

7. Deductive argument.

8. Inductive argument: a prediction.

9. Inductive argument: an argument from analogy.

10. Deductive argument.

1. Weak inductive argument.

2. Valid deductive argument. It is based on the fact that a standard deck of playing cards has 52 cards in it and that 52 minus 1 is 51.

3. Fairly strong inductive argument.

4. Valid deductive argument.

5. Weak inductive argument.

6. Valid deductive argument.

7. Invalid deductive argument.

8. Weak inductive argument. Since there are many colors in the spectrum that are not red and only one color (namely, red itself) that is red, it is not likely that John's favorite color is red.

9. Weak inductive argument.

10. Strong inductive argument.

1.5

1. This argument has the form

> All *F* are *V*.
> All *V* are *A*.
> Therefore, all *F* are *A*.

This is a valid argument form and every substitution instance of it, including the given one, is valid.

2. This argument has the form

> All *F* are *V*.
> Some *B* are *F*.
> Therefore, some *B* are *V*.

This is a valid argument form and every substitution instance of it, including the given one, is valid.

3. This argument has the form

> All *F* are *V*.
> Some *B* are *V*.
> Therefore, some *B* are *F*.

This is an invalid argument form. It has the following substitution instance in which the premises are true and the conclusion is false:

> All fish are vertebrates.
> Some bears are vertebrates.
> Therefore, some bears are fish.

4. This argument has the form

> No *G* are *B*.
> All *M* are *B*.
> Therefore, no *G* are *M*.

This is a valid argument form; all substitution instances of it are valid, including the given one.

5. This argument has the form

> No *G* are *B*.
> Some *M* are *B*.
> Therefore, no *M* are *G*.

This is an invalid argument form. It has the following substitution instance in which the premises are true and the conclusion is false:

> No plants are animals.
> Some living things are animals.
> Therefore, no living things are plants.

6. This argument has the form

> Some L are *P*.
> Some *L* are *M*.
> Therefore, some *P* are *M*.

This is an invalid argument form. It has the following substitution instance in which the premises are true and the conclusion is false:

> Some animals are dogs.
> Some animals are cats.
> Therefore, some dogs are cats.

7. This argument has the form

> Some *M* are *E*.
> All *G* are *M*.
> Therefore, some *E* are *G*.

This is an invalid argument form. It has the following substitution instance in which the premises are true and the conclusion is false:

> Some human beings are females.
> All men are human beings.
> Therefore, some females are men.

8. This argument has the form

> Some *L* are *T*.
> No *J* are *L*.
> Therefore, some *T* are not *J*.

This is a valid argument form and every substitution instance of it, including the given one, is valid.

9. This argument has the form

> All *B* are *D*.
> No *D* are *F*.
> Therefore, no *B* are *F*.

This is a valid argument form and all substitution instances of it, including the given one, are valid.

10. This argument has the form

> All *T* are *C*.
> All *T* are *B*.
> Therefore, all *C* are *B*.

This is an invalid argument form. It has the following substitution instance in which the premises are true and the conclusion is false:

> All dogs are animals.
> All dogs are mammals.
> Therefore, all animals are mammals.

1.6

1.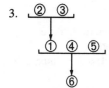

2.

3.

4.

5.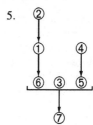

CHAPTER 2

2.1

1. positive; horse
2. negative; horse
3. negative; lawyer
4. negative; doctor
5. negative; woman, older woman
6. negative; alcoholic
7. positive; elderly person
8. negative; athlete
9. positive; minister, priest, rabbi
10. positive; gun

2.2

1. Human being, professional person, doctor, surgeon.

2. Pecan tree, tree, plant, living thing.

3. Peach tree, fruit tree, tree, plant.

4. Physical object, tool, wrench, metric wrench, box-end wrench.

5. This is a series of increasing intension and decreasing extension.

6. Triangle: three-sided plane figure.
   Right triangle: three-sided plane figure, containing one right angle.
   Isosceles triangle: three-sided plane figure, two sides of equal length.
   Equilateral triangle: three-sided plane figure, all three sides of equal length.

7. The extension of "ghost" is empty, i.e., the empty class.
   The extension of "number that equals its own square" is the number 1, i.e., the class
      containing only the number 1. (Zero is not counted as a number.)
   The extension of "last king of France" is Louis-Philippe, i.e., the class containing only
      Louis-Philippe.
   The extension of "rational number whose square is 2" is empty, i.e., the empty class.
   The extension of "perfect square number between 1 and 100" is 1, 4, 9, 16, 25, 36, 49,
      64, 81, and 100 (i.e., the set containing these numbers), provided that "between" is
      understood inclusively. If "between" is understood exclusively, then 1 and 100 are
      not included.

8. a. Plane figure, polygon, less than five sides, etc.
   b. Plane figure, polygon, all sides of equal length, etc.
   c. Animal, mammal, four-legged, etc.
   d. Material object, useful object, etc.

9. Whole number between 1.2 and 1.25; king of France in 1980; mother of Adam; first man
   on the moon in 1950; unicorn.

10. First man on the moon; whole number between 1 and 3; President of the United States in
    1987; father of Isaac; author of *A Concise Introduction to Logic.*

1. Religion is the opiate of the masses.
   Religion is the supreme road to happiness.

2. This is both a stipulative definition (since the word "entropy" is first given a meaning by it) and a theoretical definition (since it is defined in terms of the theory and has logical implications for the theory).

3. This is a stipulative definition. Insofar as it is part of a mathematical theory, it is also a theoretical definition.

4. This is a persuasive definition (since it is intended to create a positive attitude toward death).

5. This is a lexical definition.

2.4

1. A square is a rectangle with all sides of equal length.
   A circle is a plane figure in which every point is equidistant from some fixed point.
   An even number is a whole number evenly divisible by 2.
   An odd number is a whole number not evenly divisible by 2.

2. This is an operational definition.

3. This is a definition by subclass.

4. This is an ostensive or demonstrative definition.

5. An entity is ductile if and only if, when it is pulled from two opposite directions, it stretches without breaking. An entity is malleable if and only if, when it is hammered, it flattens without cracking.

6. A marsupial is a kangaroo, a possum, and the like.
   An ungulate is a horse, a cow, a goat, and the like.

7. No. Stipulative definitions that are part of a theory and determine the contents of that theory are also theoretical definitions.

8. A junior college in which only courses for the first two years, the freshman and sophomore years, are offered. This is a definition by genus (college) and difference (in which only courses for the first two years are offered).

9. Mercury, Venus, Earth, Mars, Jupiter, Saturn, Neptune, Uranus, Pluto.

10. This is a synonymous definition.

1. This definition is too broad.

2. This definition is too narrow in that it fails to include horses that are neither ridden nor used to do work. It is also too broad in that it includes elephants, oxen, and the like. Additionally, the word "large" is vague to some extent.

3. This definition fails to indicate the context (poker) to which the definiens belongs.

4. This definition is too narrow in that it fails to include tables with three legs, for examples. It is too broad in that it includes benches and stools.

5. This definition is expressed in metaphorical and vague language.

6. The most prominent defect of this definition is its use of affective (abusive) language. It is also both too broad and too narrow, and it contains a metaphor.

7. This definition is expressed in metaphorical and vague language.

8. This definition is too broad: someone may believe something true without having any good reason for doing so. This belief would certainly not count as knowledge.

9. This definition is expressed in vague and obscure language. It may also be circular.

10. This definition of a common object is framed in obscure language. Also, it is too narrow: some balls, e.g., those used as globes or teaching devices, may not have "nonutilitarian functionality."

CHAPTER 3

3.1

1. "Miscarriage" in the first premise means a premature discharge of a fetus. In the conclusion the same word means a *breach* (of justice).

2. The premise means that people buy and eat more of Sloppy Joe's hamburgers than anyone else's hamburgers. But the conclusion "understands" the premise to mean that each one of Sloppy Joe's hamburgers has more already eaten out of it.

3. The premise is true because no matter what is done a wart will sooner or later go away (being a viral infection that the body sooner or later fights off). But this does not lead to the conclusion that killing the toad by the light of the full moon will cure warts.

4. To be a superb thief means to be superb at thieving. But to be a superb man is not to be both a man and a superb thief: it is to be a man with excellent qualities, especially of the moral sort. That is, "superb" is used in different senses.

5. "Heavy-hearted" does not mean with a (literally) heavy heart. It means sad and downcast.

3.2

1. Straw man
2. Ad populum
3. Ad populum
4. Accident
5. Missing the point: This is a matter of equal *rights*, not equal size.
6. Accident
7. Accident
8. Ad hominem abusive
9. Ad hominem circumstantial
10. Appeal to pity
11. Missing the point: This is a question of morals, not actual behavior.
12. Appeal to pity
13. Appeal to pity
14. Appeal to force
15. Accident
16. Appeal to force
17. Ad hominem circumstantial
18. Missing the point
19. Ad hominem (tu quoque version)
20. Ad populum. Despite the fact that the appeal is to be different from the crowd, it is still an appeal to the person's vanity or self-esteem.

3.3

1. false cause
2. false cause
3. hasty generalization
4. appeal to unqualified authority
5. appeal to ignorance
6. false cause
13. false cause (or: weak analogy)
14. weak analogy
15. hasty generalization
16. appeal to ignorance
7. false cause
8. appeal to ignorance
9. slippery slope
10. weak analogy
11. slippery slope
12. weak analogy
17. false cause
18. appeal to unqualified authority
19. hasty generalization
20. false cause

3.4

1. Equivocation (on "arms")
2. Division
3. Begging the question
4. Amphiboly
5. Amphiboly
6. Complex question
7. False dichotomy
8. Amphiboly
9. Equivocation (on "you'll never eat anyplace else again")
10. Amphiboly
11. Equivocation (on "glued to his seat")
12. Division
13. Equivocation (on "had" and on "seasoned")
14. Division
15. This is difficult to assess but is probably best assessed as equivocation (on "normalcy"). The word "normalcy" does not change meaning in one sense in this example, but in

another sense, normalcy for cats and dogs is not the same notion as normalcy for birds or people.

16. Composition
17. Amphiboly
18. Division
19. Equivocation (on "light")
20. Composition

3.5

1. Slippery slope.
2. Weak analogy.
3. Red herring.
4. Suppressed evidence.
5. Suppressed evidence
6. Weak analogy.
7. Suppressed evidence.
8. Slippery slope.
9. Weak analogy.
10. Weak analogy.

11. Slippery slope.
12. Straw man.
13. Red herring.
14. Red herring.
15. Suppressed evidence.
16. Straw man.
17. Weak analogy.
18. Weak analogy.
19. Weak analogy.
20. Slippery slope.

CHAPTER 4

4.4

1. Some fish are non-bass.
2. All non-principalities are non-angels.
3. All non-butterflies are ants.
4. All perfect things are non-mortals.
5. Some cats are non-dogs.

6. No non-gods are non-idols.
7. No non-wives are workers.
8. All non-insects are non-spiders.
9. Some poets are not authors.
10. Some wolves are females.

4.5

1. "All men are mortals." This is true. The corresponding propositions are computed as

    I: true   **E:** false   **O:** false

2. "Some fish are not bass." This is true. The corresponding propositions are computed as

    A: false   **E:** undetermined   **I:** undetermined

3. "No dogs are cats." This is true. The corresponding propositions are computed as

    A: false   **I:** false   **O:** true

4. "Some chairs are antiques." This is true. The corresponding propositions are computed as

    A: undetermined   **E:** false   **O:** undetermined

5. "Some grasshoppers are not insects." This is false. The corresponding propositions are computed as

        A: true   **I:** true   **E:** false

6. "All numbers are even numbers." This is false. The corresponding propositions are computed as

        E: undetermined   **I:** undetermined   **O:** true

7. "No authors are poets." This is false. The corresponding propositions are computed as

        A: undetermined   **I.** true   **O:** undetermined

8. "Some horses are palominos." This is true. The corresponding propositions are

        A: undetermined   **E:** false   **O:** undetermined

9. "No roses are plants." This is false. The corresponding propositions are computed as

        A: undetermined   **I:** true   **O:** undetermined

10. "Some elms are not trees." This is false. The corresponding propositions are computed as

        A: true   **E:** false   **I:** true

4.7

1. All survivors are strong things.

2. No persons who are not in the club are persons who are allowed to vote.

3. All places to which you go are places to which I will follow you.

4. All tigers are fierce things.

5. All men who will be promoted are sergeants.

6. All men who will be promoted are sergeants.

7. All elephants are big animals.

8. All non-miscreants are persons who will go unpunished, and no miscreants are persons who will go unpunished.

9. All persons identical with George Washington are persons who were the first U.S. President.

10. All persons identical with my father are persons who were carpenters.

11. Some men (*or:* some men who are near this place) are men who are at work (*or:* are men who are at this time at work).

12. All whales are mammals.

13. All times in the future are times when I will meet you.

14. No dogs are five-legged things.

15. All men who are well-fed are men who are content.

16. No persons are persons who like broccoli.

17. All persons who like broccoli are persons who love spinach. (This translation assumes that the word "you" in the proposition is used impersonally. If it is used personally, then the translation should be: All persons identical with you who like broccoli are persons who love spinach.)

18. All cities that have industry are prosperous cities.

19. Some people are people who did not like the movie.

20. All times identical to the time when you first called are times when I was surprised.

CHAPTER 5

5.1.I

1. All *P* are *M*.
   Some *S* are *M*.
   ———————
   Some *S* are *P*.   *invalid*

2. All *M* are *P*.
   All *M* are *S*.
   ———————
   All *S* are *P*.   *invalid*

3. No *P* are *M*.
   Some *M* are *S*.
   ———————
   Some *S* are not *P*.   *valid*

4. Some *M* are *P*.
   No *S* are *M*.
   ———————
   All *S* are *P*.   *invalid*

5. Some *P* are not *M*.
   Some *S* are not *M*.
   ———————
   Some *S* are not *P*.   *invalid*

6. No *P* are *M*.
   All *S* are *M*.
   ———————
   No *S* are *P*.   *valid*

7. All *P* are *M*.
   Some *M* are not *S*.
   ———————
   Some *S* are not *P*.   *invalid*

8. No *M* are *P*.
   No *M* are *S*.
   ———————
   Some *S* are not *P*.   *invalid*

9. No *M* are *P*.
   Some *S* are not *M*.
   ———————
   Some *S* are not *P*.   *invalid*

10. No *P* are *M*.
    All *M* are *S*.
    ———————
    No *S* are *P*.   *invalid*

5.1.II

1. *P* = men
   S = continents
   M = islands

   This argument is of forms **EAO**-4. It is invalid. (On the assumption that islands exist, it is valid.)

2. *P* = men
   S = continents
   M = islands

   This argument is of form **EIO**-3. It is valid.

140

3. P = seals
   S = tigers
   M = walruses

   This argument is of form **IEO**-4. It is invalid.

4. P = large animals
   S = elephants
   M = pachyderms

   In standard form the argument becomes:

   > Some pachyderms are not large animals.
   > All elephants are pachyderms.
   > _____
   > Some elephants are not large animals

   This argument is of form **OAO**-1. It is invalid.

5. P = felines
   S = dogs
   M = cats

   In standard form the argument becomes:

   > All cats are felines.
   > No dogs are cats.
   > _____
   > No dogs are felines.

   This argument is of form **AEE**-1. It is invalid.

6. P = dogs
   S = spaniels
   M = cockers

   This argument is of form I**AO**-4. It is invalid.

7. P = stallions
   S = horses
   M = roans

   In standard form the argument becomes:

   > All roans are stallions.
   > Some horses are roans.
   > _____
   > Some horses are stallions.

   This argument is of form **AII**-1. It is valid.

8. P = insects
   S = grasshoppers
   M = ants

   In standard form the argument becomes:

   > No ants are insects.
   > All ants are grasshoppers.
   > _____
   > No grasshoppers are insects.

   This argument is of form **EAE**-3. It is invalid.

9. P = paintings
    S = art objects
    M = figurines

In standard form the argument becomes:

> No paintings are figurines.
> All figurines are art objects.
> ———
> Some art objects are not paintings.

This argument is of form **EAO**-4. It is invalid. (On the assumption that figurines exist, it is valid.)

10. P = racers
    S = drivers
    M = speeders

In standard form the argument becomes:

> All racers are speeders.
> No speeders are drivers.
> ———
> No drivers are racers.

This argument is of form **AEE**-4. It is valid.

5.2.I

1. Invalid

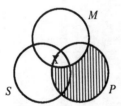

2. Invalid

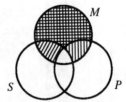

3. Valid

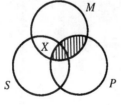

4. Invalid

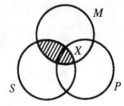

5. Invalid

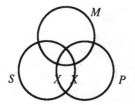

6. Valid

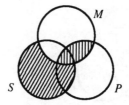

7. Invalid

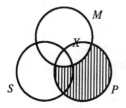

8. Invalid

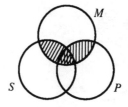

9. Invalid

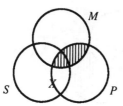

10. Invalid

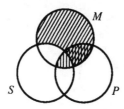

5.2.II

1. Invalid (valid existentially)

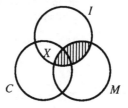

2. Valid

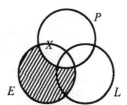

3. Invalid

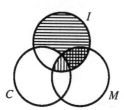

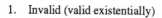

4. Invalid

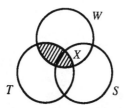

5. Invalid

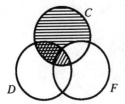

6. Invalid

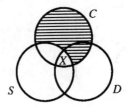

7. Valid

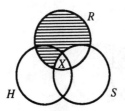

8. Invalid

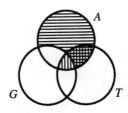

9. Invalid (valid existentially)

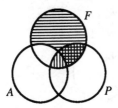

10. Valid

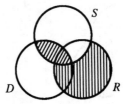

5.3

1. All *P* are *M*.
   All *M* are *S*.
   All *S* are *P*.

   S is distributed in the conclusion but not in the minor premise, so this commits the fallacy of illicit minor.

2. All *M* are *P*.
   All *S* are *M*.
   All *S* are *P*.

   This argument is valid.

3. No *P* are *M*.
   Some *S* are *M*.
   Some *S* are *P*.

   This argument commits the fallacy of drawing an affirmative conclusion from a negative premise.

4. No *M* are *P*.
   No *M* are *S*.
   No *S* are *P*.

   Having two negative premises, this argument commits the fallacy of exclusive premises.

5. All *M* are *P*
   Some *M* are *S*.
   Some *S* are *P*.

   This argument is valid.

6. Some *P* are not *M*.
   All *M* are *S*.
   Some *S* are not *P*.

   P is distributed in the conclusion but not in the major premise, so this argument commits the fallacy of illicit major.

7. Some *M* are *P*.
   No *S* are *M*.
   All *S* are *P*.

   This argument commits the fallacy of drawing an affirmative conclusion from a negative premise.

8. All *M* are *P*.
   No *M* are *S*.
   All *S* are *P*.

   This argument commits the fallacy of drawing an affirmative conclusion from a negative premise.

9. All *M* are *P*.
   No *S* are *M*.
   No *S* are *P*.

   P is distributed in the conclusion but not in the major premise, so this argument commits the fallacy of illicit major.

10. Some *M* are *P*.
    All *M* are *S*.
    Some *S* are *P*.

    This argument is valid.

5.4

1. With *P* = sane persons, *S* = financiers, and *M* = persons, this equivalent to **AII**-1. It is valid.

2. With *P* = valid arguments, *S* = chains of reasoning, and *M* = intelligible arguments, this is equivalent to **AIO**-2. It is invalid.

3. With *P* = solvent persons, *S* = happy persons, and *M* = bankers, this is equivalent to **OEO**-3. It is invalid.

4. With *P* = snacks, *S* = nutritious foods, and *M* = fattening foods, this is equivalent to **AEE**-4. It is valid.

5. With *P* = felons, *S* = scholars, and *M* = innocent persons, this is equivalent to **EIO**-2. It is valid.

5.5

1. All drinks are things that I like.
   All things identical to this one are drinks.
   All things identical to this one are things that I like.

   This is the syllogism **AAA**-1. It is valid.

2. All times you go to town are times you buy a dress.
   All times identical to today are times you go to town.
   All times identical to today are times you buy a dress.

   This is the syllogism **AAA**-1. It is valid.

3. No immoral acts are fattening acts.
    All acts of overeating are fattening acts.
    No acts of overeating are immoral acts.

    This is the syllogism **EAE**-2. It is valid.

4. All places you will go are places to which I will follow you.
    No places identical with Bali are places to which I will follow you.
    No places identical with Bali are places you will go.

    This is the syllogism **AEE**-2. It is valid.

5. All bits of money you have are bits of money we will spend.
    Some bits of money you have are ill-gotten gains.
    Some ill-gotten gains are bits of money we will spend.

    This is the syllogism **AII**-3. It is valid.

CHAPTER 6

6.1

1. ~(A · B)
2. ~A · ~B
3. (~A ∨ ~C) · B
4. ~(A ∨ B)
5. (A ∨ B) ⊃ ~C

6. A ⊃ (B · ~C)
7. ~A ≡ (B · C)
8. ~A ⊃ (~B · ~C)
9. A ≡ ~(B · C)
10. A ⊃ (~C ⊃ B)

6.2

1.   A ⊃ (B ⊃ X)
        T   T   F

2.   ~A ∨ [X ⊃ (~X)]
        F T   F   T F

3.   (A ≡ X) ≡ (B ≡ Y)
        T   F   T   F

4.   (A ≡ Z) ≡ (X ≡ Y)
        T   F   F   F

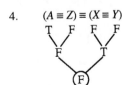

5. $X \supset \sim(X \supset \sim X)$

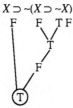

6. $(A \vee X) \supset (Y \vee Z)$

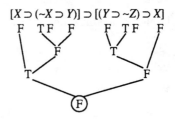

7. $[(A \cdot B) \cdot C] \equiv [A \cdot (X \vee Y)]$

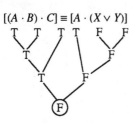

8. $[(\sim A) \equiv (\sim X)] \vee (Y \vee C)$

9. $[(X \supset Y) \supset \sim Y] \supset (\sim X)$

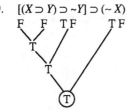

10. $[X \supset (\sim X \supset Y)] \supset [(Y \supset \sim Z) \supset X]$

6.3.I (The truth tables will be omitted in these answers.)

1. Tautology.
2. Contingency.
3. Self-contradiction.
4. Contingency.
5. Contingency.

6. Tautology.
7. Tautology.
8. Self-contradiction.
9. Contingency.
10. Contingency.

6.3.II

1. Not logically equivalent.   Inconsistent.
2. Logically equivalent.   Consistent.
3. Not logically equivalent.   Consistent.
4. Logically equivalent.   Consistent.
5. Logically equivalent.   Consistent.

<u>6.4</u> (Truth tables omitted.)

1. Valid.
2. Valid.
3. Invalid.
4. Valid.
5. Invalid.

6. Invalid.
7. Valid.
8. Invalid.
9. Valid.
10. Valid.

<u>6.5</u>

1. Valid.

2. Valid.

3. Valid.

4. Valid.

5. Invalid. P false and Q true will make the premises true and the conclusion false.

6. Valid.

7. Valid.

8. Valid.

9. Invalid. P true and Q false will make the premises true and the conclusion false.

10. Invalid. Either P true and Q false or P false and Q true will make the premise true and the conclusions false.

<u>6.6</u>

1. *Modus ponens.*
2. *Modus tollens.*
3. Disjunctive syllogism.
4. Hypothetical syllogism.
5. Constructive dilemma.

6. Destructive dilemma.
7. *Modus ponens.*
8. *Modus tollens.*
9. Disjunctive syllogism.
10. Hypothetical syllogism.

CHAPTER 7

<u>7.1</u>

(1) 4. $Y \supset Z$ 1, 2; MP
    5. Z 3, 4; MP

(2) 4. $Y \lor Z$ 1, 2; DS
    5. Z 3, 4; DS

(3) 4. $\sim Y$ 1, 2; DS
    5. $\sim Z$ 3, 4; MT

(4) 5. X 2, 3; MP
    6. $Y \lor Z$ 1, 5; MP
    7. Z 4, 6; DS

(5)	4.	X	2, 3; DS
	5.	$\sim Y \supset \sim Z$	1, 4; MP
	6.	$\sim Z$	2, 5; MP

(6)	4.	$X \supset Z$	1, 2; HS
	5.	$\sim X$	3, 4; MT

(7)	5.	X	3, 4; DS
	6.	$Y \supset Z$	1, 5; MP
	7.	$Z \supset W$	2, 5; MP
	8.	$Y \supset W$	6, 7; HS

(8)	5.	$\sim X$	3, 4; MT
	6.	$Y \cdot Z$	1, 5; DS
	7.	W	2, 6; MP

(9)	5.	$\sim \sim X$	2, 3; MT
	6.	$\sim Y$	1, 5; DS
	7.	W	4, 6; DS

(10)	5.	$X \supset \sim Y$	1, 3; MP
	6.	$\sim Y$	3, 5; MP
	7.	$\sim T$	2, 6; DS
	8.	$\sim W$	4, 7; MT

7.2

(1)	4.	$X \vee Y$	3; Add
	5.	Z	1, 4; MP
	6.	$Z \vee T$	5; Add
	7.	W	2, 6; MP

(2)	5.	X	3, 4; MP
	6.	$Y \cdot Z$	1, 5; MP
	7.	Y	6; Simp
	8.	K	2, 7; MP

(3)	5.	$Y \vee Z$	1, 4; MP
	6.	$(Y \supset W) \cdot (Z \supset K)$	2, 3; Conj
	7.	$W \vee K$	5, 6; CD

(4)	4.	$\sim Y$	3; Simp
	5.	$\sim X$	1, 4; MT
	6.	$\sim X \vee W$	5; Add
	7.	K	2, 6; MP
	8.	$K \vee T$	7; Add

(5)	4.	$\sim X$	3; Simp
	5.	$\sim Y$	2; Simp
	6.	$Y \vee Z$	1, 4; DS
	7.	Z	5, 6; DS
	8.	$Z \vee T$	7; Add

(6)	4.	$K \cdot L$	2; Simp
	5.	K	4; Simp
	6.	$X \vee Z$	3, 5; MP
	7.	$Y \vee W$	1, 6; CD

(7)	4.	$X \supset Y$	1; Simp
	5.	$Y \supset Z$	2; Simp
	6.	$X \supset Z$	4, 5; HS
	7.	$(X \supset Y) \supset W$	3, 6; MP
	8.	W	4, 7; MP

(8)	5.	$\sim L$	3; Simp
	6.	$\sim (X \cdot Y)$	2, 5; MT
	7.	$Z \cdot W$	1, 6; DS
	8.	Z	7; Simp
	9.	$N \cdot O$	4, 8; MP
	10.	N	9; Simp

(9)	5.	$X \supset Y$	1; Simp
	6.	X	2; Simp
	7.	Y	5, 6; MP
	8.	M	3, 5; MP
	9.	$Y \cdot M$	7, 8; Conj
	10.	$Z \cdot K$	4, 9; MP
	11.	Z	10; Simp
	12.	$Z \vee W$	11; Add

(10)	5.	X	2; Simp
	6.	P	1, 5; MP
	7.	$Q \cdot S$	3, 6; MP
	8.	Q	7; Simp
	9.	$P \cdot Q$	6, 8; Conj
	10.	$P \equiv Q$	4, 9; MP

(11)	4.	A	2; Simp
	5.	$B \supset C$	1, 4; MP
	6.	B	3; Simp
	7.	C	5, 6; MP
	8.	$C \cdot A$	4, 7; Conj

(12)	5.	$\sim X$	3; Simp
	6.	$\sim A$	2, 5; MT
	7.	$\sim(B \supset C)$	1, 6; MT
	8.	$\sim D$	4, 7; MT
	9.	$\sim A \cdot \sim D$	6, 8; Conj

(13)	5.	$A \supset B$	1; Simp
	6.	$B \supset E$	2; Simp
	7.	$A \supset E$	5, 6; HS
	8.	$H \cdot I$	3, 7; MP
	9.	H	8; Simp
	10.	J	4, 9; MP
	11.	$H \cdot J$	9, 10; Conj

(14)	6.	A	4; Simp
	7.	B	3, 6; MP
	8.	$A \cdot B$	6, 7; Conj
	9.	$C \vee D$	1, 8; MP
	10.	$D \supset G$	5; Simp
	11.	$(C \supset E) \cdot (D \supset G)$	2, 10; Conj
	12.	$E \vee G$	9, 11; CD
	13.	$(A \cdot B) \cdot (E \vee G)$	8, 12; Conj

(15)	5.	$\sim C$	3, 4; MT
	6.	A	2, 5; DS
	7.	B	1, 6; MP
	8.	$B \cdot \sim C$	5, 7; Conj
	9.	$(B \cdot \sim C) \vee E$	8; Add

7.3

(1)	4.	$\sim X \vee \sim Y$	1; DM
	5.	$\sim \sim X$	2; DN
	6.	$\sim Y$	4, 5; DS
	7.	Z	3, 6; DS

(2)	4.	$(X \cdot Y) \vee (X \cdot Z)$	1; Dist
	5.	$X \cdot Z$	2, 4; DS
	6.	$Z \cdot X$	5; Com
	7.	K	3, 6; MP

(3)	4.	X	3; Simp
	5.	$\sim \sim X$	4; DN
	6.	Y	1, 5; DS
	7.	$\sim \sim Y$	6; DN
	8.	Z	2, 7; DS
	9.	$X \cdot Y$	4, 6; Conj
	10.	$(X \cdot Y) \cdot Z$	8, 9; Conj

(4)	3.	$\sim Z \cdot \sim W$	2; DM
	4.	$\sim Z$	3; Simp
	5.	$\sim(X \vee Y)$	1, 4; MT
	6.	$\sim X \cdot \sim Y$	5; DM
	7.	$\sim Y \cdot \sim X$	6; Com
	8.	$\sim Y$	7; Simp

(5) 4. X 1; Simp
     5. $(Y \cdot Z) \cdot X$ 1; Com
     6. $Y \cdot Z$ 5; Simp
     7. Y 6; Simp
     8. $Z \cdot Y$ 6; Com
     9. Z 8; Simp
    10. $Y \cdot X$ 4, 7; Conj
    11. $W \cdot T$ 2, 10; MP
    12. W 11; Simp
    13. $Y \cdot W$ 7, 12; Conj
    14. $(Y \cdot W) \cdot Z$ 9, 13; Conj

(6) 4. $\sim T \cdot W$ 2; Com
     5. $\sim T$ 4; Simp
     6. $\sim\sim X$ 1, 5; MT
     7. X 6; DN
     8. $X \vee Y$ 7; Add
     9. Z 3, 8; MP
    10. W 2; Simp
    11. $W \cdot Z$ 9, 10; Conj

(7) 3. $\sim X \vee \sim Y$ 1; Add
     4. $\sim(X \cdot Y)$ 3; DM
     5. $\sim W$ 2, 4; MP
     6. $\sim W \vee \sim Z$ 5; Add
     7. $\sim(W \cdot Z)$ 6; DM

(8) 2. $\sim X \cdot \sim\sim X$ 1; DM
     3. $\sim X$ 2; Simp
     4. $\sim\sim X \cdot \sim X$ 2; Com
     5. $\sim\sim X$ 4; Simp
     6. X 5; DN
     7. $X \vee Y$ 6; Add
     8. Y 3, 7; DS

(9) 4. $X \vee \sim Y$ 1; Add
     5. $\sim Y \vee X$ 4; Com
     6. Z 2, 5; MP
     7. $X \cdot Z$ 1, 6; Conj
     8. $\sim\sim(X \cdot Z)$ 7; DN
     9. W 3, 8; DS
    10. $W \cdot X$ 1, 9; Conj
    11. $(W \cdot X) \cdot Z$ 6, 10; Conj

(10) 3. X 1; Simp
     4. $X \vee Y$ 3; Add
     5. $Y \vee X$ 4; Com
     6. $\sim W$ 2, 5; MP
     7. $\sim Z \cdot X$ 1; Com
     8. $\sim Z$ 7; Simp
     9. $\sim Z \cdot \sim W$ 6, 8; Conj
    10. $\sim(Z \vee W)$ 9; DM

151

(1)	3. $X \vee \sim Y$	1; Add
	4. $\sim Y \vee X$	3; Com
	5. $Y \supset X$	4; Impl
	6. Z	2, 5; MP
	7. $X \cdot Z$	1, 6; Conj
(2)	3. $\sim X \vee Y$	1; Impl
	4. $Y \vee \sim X$	3; Com
	5. $Y \supset Z$	2, 4; MP
	6. $X \supset Z$	1, 5; HS
	7. $\sim Z \supset \sim X$	6; Trans
(3)	3. $X \cdot Y$	1, 2; Conj
	4. $(X \cdot Y) \vee (\sim X \cdot \sim Y)$	3; Add
	5. $X \equiv Y$	4; Equiv
(4)	3. $X \vee Y$	1; Add
	4. $Y \vee X$	3; Com
	5. $\sim\sim Y \vee X$	4; DN
	6. $\sim Y \supset X$	5; Impl
	7. $(X \supset \sim Y) \cdot (\sim Y \supset X)$	2, 6; Conj
	8. $X \equiv \sim Y$	
(5)	3. $\sim X \vee Y$	1; Impl
	4. $\sim X \vee Z$	2; Impl
	5. $(\sim X \vee Y) \cdot (\sim X \vee Z)$	3, 4; Conj
	6. $\sim X \vee (Y \cdot Z)$	5; Dist
	7. $X \supset (Y \cdot Z)$	6; Impl
(6)	2. $\sim X \vee (Y \cdot Z)$	1; Impl
	3. $(\sim X \vee Y) \cdot (\sim X \vee Z)$	2; Dist
	4. $(X \supset Y) \cdot (\sim X \vee Z)$	3; Impl
	5. $(X \supset Y) \cdot (X \supset Z)$	4; Impl
(7)	3. $\sim X \vee Z$	1; Impl
	4. $\sim Y \vee Z$	2; Impl
	5. $Z \vee \sim X$	3; Com
	6. $Z \vee \sim Y$	4; Com
	7. $(Z \vee \sim X) \cdot (Z \vee \sim Y)$	5, 6; Conj
	8. $Z \vee (\sim X \cdot \sim Y)$	7; Dist
	9. $Z \vee \sim(X \vee Y)$	8; DM
	10. $\sim(X \vee Y) \vee Z$	9; Com
	11. $(X \vee Y) \supset Z$	10; Impl
(8)	2. $\sim(X \vee Y) \vee Z$	1; Impl
	3. $Z \vee \sim(X \vee Y)$	2; Com
	4. $Z \vee (\sim X \cdot \sim Y)$	3; DM
	5. $(Z \vee \sim X) \cdot (Z \vee \sim Y)$	4; Dist
	6. $(\sim X \vee Z) \cdot (Z \vee \sim Y)$	5; Com

7.	$(\sim X \vee Z) \cdot (\sim Y \vee Z)$	6; Com
8.	$(X \supset Z) \cdot (\sim Y \vee Z)$	7; Impl
9.	$(X \supset Z) \cdot (Y \supset Z)$	8; Impl

(9) 3.	$\sim X \vee (X \cdot Y)$	1; Impl
4.	$(\sim X \vee X) \cdot (\sim X \vee Y)$	3; Dist
5.	$\sim X \vee X$	4; Simp
6.	$X \vee \sim X$	5; Com
7.	$[(Y \cdot X) \vee (\sim X \cdot Y)] \supset Y$	2; Com
8.	$[(Y \cdot X) \vee (Y \cdot \sim X)] \supset Y$	7; Com
9.	$[Y \cdot (X \vee \sim X)] \supset Y$	8; Dist
10.	$\sim[Y \cdot (X \vee \sim X)] \vee Y$	9; Impl
11.	$Y \vee \sim[Y \cdot (X \vee \sim X)]$	10; Com
12.	$Y \vee [\sim Y \vee \sim(X \vee \sim X)]$	11; DM
13.	$(Y \vee \sim Y) \vee \sim(X \vee \sim X)$	12; Assoc
14.	$\sim(X \vee \sim X) \vee (Y \vee \sim Y)$	13; Com
15.	$(X \vee \sim X) \supset (Y \vee \sim Y)$	14; Impl
16.	$Y \vee \sim Y$	6, 15; MP
17.	$\sim Y \vee Y$	16; Com
18.	$Y \supset Y$	17; Impl

(10) 4.	$\sim(X \cdot Y) \vee X$	1; Impl
5.	$X \vee \sim(X \cdot Y)$	4; Com
6.	$X \vee (\sim X \vee \sim Y)$	5; Dist
7.	$(X \vee \sim X) \vee \sim Y$	6; Assoc
8.	$\sim Y \vee (X \vee \sim X)$	7; Com
9.	$\sim\sim Y$	2; DN
10.	$X \vee \sim X$	8, 9; DS
11.	$\sim X \vee X$	10; Com
12.	$X \supset X$	11; Impl
13.	X	3, 12; MP
14.	$X \cdot Y$	2, 13; Conj

(11) 3.	$A \supset (\sim\sim B \vee C)$	1; DN
4.	$A \supset (\sim B \supset C)$	3; Impl
5.	$(A \cdot \sim B) \supset C$	4; Exp
6.	$(\sim B \cdot A) \supset C$	5; Com
7.	$\sim B \supset (A \supset C)$	6; Exp
8.	$A \supset C$	2, 7; MP

(12) 3.	$\sim A \vee (B \vee C)$	1; Impl
4.	$\sim A \vee (C \vee B)$	3; Com
5.	$(\sim A \vee C) \vee B$	4; Assoc
6.	$\sim\sim(\sim A \vee C) \vee B$	5; DN
7.	$\sim(\sim A \vee C) \supset B$	6; Impl
8.	$\sim(\sim A \vee C) \supset C$	2, 7; HS
9.	$\sim\sim(\sim A \vee C) \vee C$	8; Impl
10.	$(\sim A \vee C) \vee C$	9; DN
11.	$\sim A \vee (C \vee C)$	10; Assoc
12.	$\sim A \vee C$	11; Taut
13.	$A \supset C$	12; Impl

(13) 2. $(\sim A \lor B) \supset (B \supset A)$ 1; Impl
    3. $(\sim A \lor B) \supset (\sim B \lor A)$ 2; Impl
    4. $\sim(\sim A \lor B) \lor (\sim B \lor A)$ 3; Impl
    5. $(\sim\sim A \cdot \sim B) \lor (\sim B \lor A)$ 4; DM
    6. $(A \cdot \sim B) \lor (\sim B \lor A)$ 5; DN
    7. $(\sim B \lor A) \lor (A \cdot \sim B)$ 6; Com
    8. $[(\sim B \lor A) \lor A] \cdot [(\sim B \lor A) \lor \sim B]$ 7; Dist
    9. $(\sim B \lor A) \lor A$ 8; Simp
   10. $\sim B \lor (A \lor A)$ 9; Assoc
   11. $\sim B \lor A$ 10; Taut
   12. $B \supset A$ 11; Impl

(14) 3. $A \cdot \sim B$ 1, 2; Conj
    4. $\sim\sim A \cdot \sim B$ 3; DN
    5. $\sim(\sim A \lor B)$ 4; DM
    6. $\sim(A \supset B)$ 5; Impl
    7. $\sim(A \supset B) \lor \sim(B \supset A)$ 6; Add
    8. $\sim[(A \supset B) \cdot (B \supset A)]$ 7; DM
    9. $\sim(A \equiv B)$ 8; Equiv

(15) 3. $\sim[(A \supset B) \cdot (B \supset A)]$ 1; Equiv
    4. $\sim(A \supset B) \lor \sim(B \supset A)$ 3; DM
    5. $A \lor \sim B$ 2; Add
    6. $\sim B \lor A$ 5; Com
    7. $B \supset A$ 6; Impl
    8. $\sim\sim(B \supset A)$ 7; DN
    9. $\sim(B \supset A) \lor \sim(A \supset B)$ 4; Com
   10. $\sim(A \supset B)$ 8, 9; DS
   11. $\sim(\sim A \lor B)$ 10; Impl
   12. $\sim\sim A \cdot \sim B$ 11; DM
   13. $\sim B \cdot \sim\sim A$ 12; Com
   14. $\sim B$ 13; Simp

(16) 2. $\sim[(A \cdot B) \lor (\sim A \cdot \sim B)]$ 1; Equiv
    3. $\sim(A \cdot B) \cdot \sim(\sim A \cdot \sim B)$ 2; DM
    4. $(\sim A \lor \sim B) \cdot (\sim\sim A \lor \sim\sim B)$ 3; DM, DM
    5. $(\sim A \lor \sim B) \cdot (\sim\sim A \lor B)$ 4; DN
    6. $(\sim\sim A \lor B) \cdot (\sim A \lor \sim B)$ 5; Com
    7. $(\sim\sim A \lor B) \cdot (\sim B \lor \sim A)$ 6; Com
    8. $(\sim A \supset B) \cdot (B \supset \sim A)$ 7; Impl, Impl
    9. $\sim A \equiv B$ 8; Equiv

(17) 2. $\sim[(A \cdot B) \lor (\sim A \cdot \sim B)]$ 1; Equiv
    3. $\sim(A \cdot B) \cdot \sim(\sim A \cdot \sim B)$ 2; DM
    4. $(\sim A \lor \sim B) \cdot (\sim\sim A \lor \sim\sim B)$ 3; DM, DM
    5. $(\sim A \lor \sim B) \cdot (\sim\sim B \lor \sim\sim A)$ 4; Com
    6. $(\sim A \lor \sim B) \cdot (\sim\sim B \lor A)$ 5; DN
    7. $(A \supset \sim B) \cdot (\sim B \supset A)$ 6; Impl, Impl
    8. $A \equiv \sim B$ 7; Equiv

(18)	3.	$\sim(\sim A \lor B)$	1; Impl
	4.	$\sim\sim A \cdot \sim B$	3; DM
	5.	$\sim\sim A$	4; Simp
	6.	$\sim(\sim C \lor D)$	2; Impl
	7.	$\sim\sim C \cdot \sim D$	6; DM
	8.	$\sim D \cdot \sim\sim C$	7; Com
	9.	$\sim D$	8; Simp
	10.	$\sim\sim A \cdot \sim D$	5, 9; Conj
	11.	$\sim(\sim A \lor D)$	10; DM
	12.	$\sim(A \supset D)$	11; Impl

(19)	3.	$\sim(\sim A \lor B)$	1; Impl
	4.	$\sim\sim A \cdot \sim B$	3; DM
	5.	$\sim B \cdot \sim\sim A$	4; Com
	6.	$\sim B$	5; Simp
	7.	$\sim(\sim B \lor C)$	2; Impl
	8.	$\sim\sim B \cdot \sim C$	7; DM
	9.	$\sim\sim B$	8; Simp
	10.	$\sim B \lor (A \supset C)$	6; Add
	11.	$A \supset C$	9, 10; DS

(20)	3.	$\sim[(A \cdot B) \lor (\sim A \cdot \sim B)]$	1; Equiv
	4.	$\sim(A \cdot B) \cdot \sim(\sim A \cdot \sim B)$	3; DM
	5.	$(\sim A \lor \sim B) \cdot (\sim\sim A \lor \sim\sim B)$	4; DM, DM
	6.	$(\sim A \lor \sim B)$	5; Simp
	7.	$A \supset \sim B$	6; Impl
	8.	$\sim\sim A \lor \sim\sim B$	5; Com, Simp
	9.	$A \lor \sim\sim B$	8; DN
	10.	$\sim\sim B \lor A$	9; Com
	11.	$\sim B \supset A$	10; Impl
	12.	$\sim[(B \cdot C) \lor (\sim B \cdot \sim C)]$	2; Equiv
	13.	$\sim(B \cdot C) \cdot \sim(\sim B \cdot \sim C)$	12; DM,
	14.	$(\sim B \lor \sim C) \cdot (\sim\sim B \lor \sim\sim C)$	13; DM, DM
	15.	$\sim B \lor \sim C$	14; Simp
	16.	$\sim C \lor \sim B$	15; Com
	17.	$C \supset \sim B$	16; Impl
	18.	$C \supset A$	11, 17; HS
	19.	$\sim\sim B \lor \sim\sim C$	14; Com, Simp
	20.	$\sim\sim B \lor C$	19; DN
	21.	$\sim B \supset C$	20; Impl
	22.	$A \supset C$	7, 21; HS
	23.	$(A \supset C) \cdot (C \supset A)$	18, 22; Conj
	24.	$A \equiv C$	23; Equiv

7.5

(1)
2. Y	ACP
3. $Y \lor X$	2; Add
4. $X \lor Y$	3; Com
5. $Z \cdot W$	1, 4; MP
6. $W \cdot Z$	5; Com
7. W	6; Simp
8. $Y \supset W$	2-7; CP

(2)
2. $X \cdot W$	ACP
3. X	2; Simp
4. $W \cdot X$	2; Com
5. W	4; Simp
6. $X \lor Y$	3; Add
7. $(Z \lor W) \supset R$	1, 6; MP
7. $W \lor Z$	5; Add
9. $Z \lor W$	8; Com
10. R	7, 9; MP
11. $(X \cdot W) \supset R$	2-10; CP

(3)
3. $X \lor Z$	ACP
4. $(X \supset Y) \cdot (Z \supset W)$	1, 2; Conj
5. $Y \lor W$	3, 4; CD
6. $(X \lor Z) \supset (Y \lor W)$	3-5; CP

(4)
3. $X \cdot Z$	ACP
4. X	3; Simp
5. Y	1, 4; MP
6. $Z \cdot X$	3; Com
7. Z	6; Simp
8. W	2, 7; MP
9. $Y \cdot W$	5, 8; Conj
10. $(X \cdot Z) \supset (Y \cdot W)$	3-9; CP

(5)
2. X	ACP
3. $X \lor Y$	2; Add
4. $(Z \lor W) \supset R$	1, 3; MP
5. Z	ACP
6. $Z \lor W$	5; Add
7. R	4, 6; MP
8. $Z \supset R$	5-7; CP
9. $X \supset (Z \supset R)$	2-8; CP

(6)
3. $\sim Y \cdot \sim W$	ACP
4. $\sim Y$	3; Simp
5. $\sim X$	1, 4; MT
6. $\sim W \cdot \sim Y$	3; Com
7. $\sim W$	6; Simp
8. $\sim Z$	2, 7; MT
9. $\sim X \cdot \sim Z$	5, 8; Conj
10. $(\sim Y \cdot \sim W) \supset (\sim X \cdot \sim Z)$	3-9; CP

(7)
3. X	ACP
4. $Y \cdot Z$	1, 3; MP
5. $Z \cdot Y$	4; Com
6. Z	5; Simp
7. $X \supset Z$	3-6; CP
8. Z	ACP
9. $X \cdot W$	2, 8; MP
10. X	9; Simp
11. $Z \supset X$	8-10; CP
12. $(X \supset Z) \cdot (Z \supset X)$	7, 11; Conj
13. $X \equiv Z$	12; Equiv

(8)
3. X	ACP
4. $X \lor Y$	3; Add
5. Z	1, 4; MP
6. $X \supset Z$	3-5; CP
7. $\sim X$	ACP
8. $\sim X \lor \sim L$	7; Add
9. $\sim Z \cdot \sim W$	2, 8; MP
10. $\sim Z$	9; Simp
11. $\sim X \supset \sim Z$	7-10; CP
12. $Z \supset X$	11; Trans
13. $(X \supset Z) \cdot (Z \supset X)$	6, 12; Conj
14. $X \equiv Z$	13; Equiv

(9)
3. $X \lor Z$	ACP
4. $(X \supset Y) \cdot (Z \supset Y)$	1, 2; Conj
5. $Y \lor Y$	2, 4; CD
6. Y	5; Taut
7. $(X \lor Z) \supset Y$	3-6; CP

(10) 3. $\sim X \vee \sim Y$ 1; DM

4. $\sim Y \vee \sim X$ 3; Com

5. $\sim Z \vee \sim(Y \vee W)$ 2; DM

6. $\sim Z \vee (\sim Y \cdot \sim W)$ 5; DM

7. $(\sim Z \vee \sim Y) \cdot (\sim Z \vee \sim W)$ 6; Dist

8. $\sim Z \vee \sim Y$ 7; Simp

9. $\sim Y \vee \sim Z$ 8; Com

10. Y ACP

11. $\sim\sim Y$ 10; DN

12. $\sim X$ 4, 11; DS

13. $\sim Z$ 9, 11; DS

14. $\sim X \cdot \sim Z$ 12, 13; Conj

15. $Y \supset (\sim X \cdot \sim Z)$ 10-14; CP

7.6

(1)   2. $\sim(Y \vee \sim Y)$ AIP

3. $\sim Y \cdot \sim\sim Y$ 2; DM

4. $Y \vee \sim Y$ 2-3; IP

(2)   3. $\sim(Z \vee W)$ AIP

4. $\sim Z \cdot \sim W$ 3; DM

5. $\sim Z$ 4; Simp

6. $\sim Y$ 2, 5; MT

7. $Y \cdot X$ 1; Com

8. Y 7; Simp

9. $Y \cdot \sim Y$ 6, 8; Conj

10. $Z \vee W$ 3-9; IP

(3)   3. $\sim\sim X$ AIP

4. X 3; DN

5. Y 1, 4; MP

6. $\sim Y$ 2, 5; MP

7. $Y \cdot \sim Y$ 5, 6; Conj

8. $\sim X$ 3-7; IP

(4)   4. $Z \vee \sim Y$ 3; Com

5. $\sim Z$ AIP

6. $\sim Y$ 4, 5; DS

7. $\sim X$ 2, 6; MT

8. X 1, 7; MP

9. $X \cdot \sim X$ 7, 8; Conj

10. Z 5-9; IP

(5) | U) $T \vee \sim U$)   AIP
      | 7. $\sim T \cdot \sim U$ 6; DM
      | 8. $\sim T$ 7; Simp
      | 9. $T \vee \sim Y$ 3; Com
      |10. $\sim Y$ 8, 10; DS
      |11. $\sim X$ 1, 10; MT
      |12. Z 5, 11; MP
      |13. W 2, 12; MP
      |14. $\sim U \cdot \sim T$ 7; Com
      |15. $\sim U$ 14; Simp
      |16. $\sim W$ 4, 15; MP
      |17. $W \cdot \sim W$ 13, 16; Conj
    18. $T \vee U$ 6-17; IP

7.7

(1)   / $P \supset [P \cdot (Q \vee \sim Q)]$
      | 1. P ACP
      | |2. $\sim(Q \vee \sim Q)$ AIP
      | |3. $\sim Q \cdot \sim\sim Q$ 2; DM
      | 4. $Q \vee \sim Q$ 2, 3; IP
      | 5. $P \cdot (Q \vee \sim Q)$ 1, 4; Conj
      6. $P \supset [P \cdot (Q \vee \sim Q)]$ 1, 5; CP

(2)   / $P \supset [\sim P \supset (P \vee P)]$
      | 1. P ACP
      | |2. $\sim P$ ACP
      | |3. $P \vee P$ 1; Taut
      | 4. $\sim P \supset (P \vee P)$ 2-3; CP
      5. $P \supset [\sim P \supset (P \vee P)]$ 1-4; CP

(3)   / $[(P \supset Q) \supset P] \supset P$
      | 1. $(P \supset Q) \supset P$ ACP
      | 2. $\sim(P \supset Q) \vee P$ 1; Impl
      | 3. $\sim(\sim P \vee Q) \vee P$ 2; Impl
      | 4. $(\sim\sim P \cdot \sim Q) \vee P$ 3; DM
      | 5. $(P \cdot \sim Q) \vee P$ 4; DN
      | 6. $P \vee (P \cdot \sim Q)$ 5; Com
      | 7. $(P \vee P) \cdot (P \vee \sim Q)$ 6; Dist
      | 8. $P \vee P$ 7; Simp
      | 9. P 8; Taut
    10. $[(P \supset Q) \supset P] \supset P$ 1-9; CP

(4) / $(P \supset Q) \vee (P \cdot {\sim}Q)$

    | 1. $\sim(P \supset Q)$ ACP
    | 2. $\sim({\sim}P \vee Q)$ 1; Impl
    | 3. $\sim\sim P \cdot \sim Q$ 2; DM
    | 4. $P \cdot \sim Q$ 3; DN
       5. $\sim(P \supset Q) \supset (P \cdot {\sim}Q)$ 1-4; CP
       6. $\sim\sim(P \supset Q) \vee (P \cdot {\sim}Q)$ 5; Impl
       7. $(P \supset Q) \vee (P \cdot \sim Q)$ 6; DN

(5) / $(P \vee Q) \vee [{\sim}P \cdot (Q \supset {\sim}Q)]$

    | 1. $\sim(P \vee Q)$ ACP
    | 2. $\sim P \cdot \sim Q$ 1; DM
    | 3. $\sim P$ 2; Simp
    | 4. $\sim Q \cdot \sim P$ 2; Com
    | 5. $\sim Q$ 4; Simp
    | 6. $\sim Q \vee \sim Q$ 5; Taut
    | 7. $Q \supset \sim Q$ 6; Impl
    | 8. $\sim P \cdot (Q \supset \sim Q)$ 3, 7; Conj
       9. $\sim(P \vee Q) \supset [{\sim}P \cdot (Q \supset {\sim}Q)]$ 1-8; CP
    10. $\sim\sim(P \vee Q) \vee [{\sim}P \cdot (Q \supset {\sim}Q)]$ 9; Impl
    11. $(P \vee Q) \vee [{\sim}P \cdot (Q \supset {\sim}Q)]$ 10; DN

CHAPTER 8

8.1

1. $(x)(Sx \supset Rx)$

2. $(x)[(Sx \cdot Rx) \supset Px]$

3. $(x)[(Sx \cdot Px) \supset (Rx \vee Cx)]$

4. This proposition is ambiguous. If it means that of all things only poisonous snakes are rattlers, then it is to be translated as:

    $(x)[Rx \supset (Px \cdot Sx)]$

    But if it means that of snakes only the poisonous ones are rattlers, then it is to be translated as:

    $(x)[Sx \supset (Rx \supset Px)]$

5. $(\exists x)[(Px \cdot Sx) \cdot Rx]$

6. $(x)[(Rx \cdot Px) \supset Sx]$

7. $(x)[Cx \supset (Rx \equiv {\sim}Px)]$

8. $(\exists x)[Cx \cdot (Px \supset Sx)]$

9. $(\exists x)[(Px \cdot Sx) \cdot Zx]$

10. $(x)[(Px \cdot Sx) \cdot (Dx \cdot Cx)]$

(1)   4. $Ax \supset Bx$ 1; UI
        5. $Bx \supset Cx$ 2; UI
        6. $Cx \supset Dx$ 3; UI
        7. $Ax \supset Cx$ 4, 5; HS
        8. $Ax \supset Dx$ 6, 7; HS
        9. $\sim\!Dx \supset \sim\!Ax$ 8; Trans
     10. $(x)(\sim\!Dx \supset \sim\!Ax)$ 9; UG

(2)   3. $Ac \cdot Bc$ 1; UI
        4. Ac 3; Simp
        5. $(\exists x)Ax$ 4; EG
        6. $(\exists x)Cx$ 2, 5; MP

(3)   2. $Ac \cdot Bc$ 1; EI
        3. Ac 2; Simp
        4. $(\exists x)Ax$ 3; EG
        5. $Bc \cdot Ac$ 2; Com
        6. Bc 5; Simp
        7. $(\exists x)Bx$ 6; EG
        8. $(\exists x)Ax \cdot (\exists x)Bx$ 4, 7; Conj

(4)   4. $\sim\!(x)Ax$ 2, 3; MT
        5. $(x)Bx$ 1, 4; DS
        6. Bc 5; UI
        7. $(\exists x)Bx$ 6; EG

(5)   4. $Ac \lor Bc$ 1; EI
        5. $\sim\!Ac$ 2; UI
        6. Bc 4, 5; DS
        7. $(\exists x)Bx$ 6; EG
        8. $(x)Cx$ 3, 7; MP
        9. Cx 8; UI
     10. $Cx \lor Dx$ 9; Add
     11. $(x)(Cx \lor Dx)$ 10; UG

(6)   3. $\sim\!Bc$ 2; EI
        4. $(Ac \cdot Bc) \lor Cc$ 1; UI
        5. $\sim\!Bc \lor \sim\!Ac$ 3; Add
        6. $\sim\!(Bc \cdot Ac)$ 5; DM
        7. $\sim\!(Ac \cdot Bc)$ 6; Com
        8. Cc 4, 7; DS
        9. $(\exists x)Cx$ 8; EG

(7)	5.	$Ac \lor Dc$		2; EI
	6.	$Dc \lor Ac$		5; Com
	7.	$\sim Dc$		3; UI
	8.	Ac		6, 7; DS
	9.	Bc		4; UI
	10.	$Ac \supset (Bc \supset Cc)$		1; UI
	11.	$Bc \supset Cc$		8, 10; MP
	12.	Cc		9, 11; MP
	13.	$(\exists x)Cx$		12; EG

(8)	3.	Ay		2; UI
	4.	$Ay \supset By$		1; UI
	5.	By		3, 4; MP
	6.	$(x)Bx$		5; UG

(9)	4.	$Ac \cdot Bc$		1; EI
	5.	$Bc \cdot Ac$		4; Com
	6.	Bc		5; Simp
	7.	$Bc \supset (Dc \cdot Ec)$		2; UI
	8.	$Dc \cdot Ec$		6, 7; MP
	9.	$Ec \cdot Dc$		8; Com
	10.	Ec		9; Simp
	11.	$Ec \supset \sim Fc$		3; UI
	12.	$\sim Fc$		10, 11; MP
	13.	$(\exists x)\sim Fx$		12; EG

(10)	5.	Ac		3; EI
	6.	$Ac \supset Bc$		1; UI
	7.	Bc		5, 6; MP
	8.	$\sim\sim Bc$		7; DN
	9.	$\sim Bc \lor Cc$		2; UI
	10.	Cc		8, 9; DS
	11.	$\sim Cc$		4; UI
	12.	$Cc \lor (x)Ax$		10; Add
	13.	$(x)Ax$		11, 12; DS

8.4

(1)	3.	$(x)Ax$		ACP
	4.	Ax		3; UI
	5.	$(\exists x)Ax$		4; EG
	6.	$(x)Bx$		1, 5; MP
	7.	Bx		6; UI
	8.	$(\exists x)Bx$		7; EG
	9.	$(x)Cx$		2, 8; MP
	10.	$(x)Ax \supset (x)Cx$		3-9; CP

(2)
	2. Ax	ACP
	3. $Ax \lor Bx$	3; Add
	4. $(Ax \lor Bx) \supset (Cx \cdot Dx)$	1; UI
	5. $Cx \cdot Dx$	3, 4; MP
	6. Cx	5; Simp
7.	$Ax \supset Cx$	2-6; CP
8.	$(x)(Ax \supset Cx)$	7; UG

(3)
	2. Ax	ACP
	3. $(\exists x)Ax$	2; EG
	4. $(x)(Bx \cdot Cx)$	1, 3; MP
	5. $Bx \cdot Cx$	4; UI
	6. $Cx \cdot Bx$	5; Com
	7. Cx	6; Simp
8.	$Ax \supset Cx$	2-7; CP
9.	$(x)(Ax \supset Cx)$	8; UG

(4)
	3. Bx	ACP
	4. $Bx \lor Ax$	3; Add
	5. $Ax \lor Bx$	4; Com
	6. $(\exists x)(Ax \lor Bx)$	5; EG
	7. $(x)(Cx \cdot Dx)$	1, 6; MP
	8. $Cx \cdot Dx$	7; UI
	9. $Dx \cdot Cx$	8; Com
	10. Dx	9; Simp
11.	$Bx \supset Dx$	3-10; CP
12.	$(x)(Bx \supset Dx)$	11; UG
13.	$(x)Ex$	2, 12; MP
14.	Ex	13; UI
15.	$(\exists x)Ex$	14; EG

(5)
	4. Ex	ACP
	5. $\sim\sim Ex$	4; DN
	6. $\sim\sim Ex \lor \sim Dx$	5; Add
	7. $\sim Dx \lor \sim\sim Ex$	6; Com
	8. $\sim(Dx \cdot \sim Ex)$	7; DM
	9. $Bx \supset (Dx \cdot \sim Ex)$	2; UI
	10. $\sim Bx$	8, 9; MT
	11. $\sim Bx \lor \sim Cx$	10; Add
	12. $\sim(Bx \cdot Cx)$	11; DM
	13. $(Bx \cdot Cx) \lor Ax$	1; UI
	14. Ax	12, 13; DS
	15. $Ax \supset Fx$	3; UI
	16. Fx	14, 15; MP
17.	$Ex \supset Fx$	4-16; CP
18.	$(x)(Ex \supset Fx)$	17; UG

(1) Let universe be *a, b*. Let Aa = T, Ba = T, Ab = T (or F), Bb = F. Argument becomes

　　1. $(Aa \cdot Ba) \vee (Ab \cdot Bb) / Ba \cdot Bb$

Its truth table shows the premise true and the conclusion false:

$(Aa \cdot Ba) \vee (Ab \cdot Bb) \mathbin{/\!/} Ba \cdot Bb$
T T T 　T　 T F F 　　T F F

(2) Let universe be *a, b*. Let Aa = T, Ba = T, Ca = T, Ab = F, Bb = F, Cb = T (or F). Argument becomes

　　1. $(Aa \supset Ba) \cdot (Ab \supset Bb)$
　　2. $(Aa \cdot Ca) \vee (Ab \cdot Cb) / Ba \cdot Bb$

Its truth table shows the premises true and the conclusion false:

$(Aa \supset Ba) \cdot (Ab \supset Bb) / (Aa \cdot Ca) \vee (Ab \cdot Cb) \mathbin{/\!/} Ba \cdot Bb$
T T T 　T　F T F 　　 T T T 　T　 F F T 　　 T F F

(3) Let universe be *a*. Let Aa = F, Ba = T (or F), Ca = T (or F), Da = T. Argument becomes

　　1. $Aa \supset (Ba \cdot Ca)$
　　2. $Ca \supset Da / Da \supset Aa$

Its truth table shows the premises true and the conclusion false:

$Aa \supset (Ba \cdot Ca) / Ca \supset Da \mathbin{/\!/} Da \supset Aa$
F 　T　 T T T 　　 T 　T　 T 　　 T 　F　 F

(4) Let universe be *a, b*. Let Aa = F, Ba = T (or F), Ab = T, Bb = F. Argument becomes

　　1. $(Aa \cdot Ab) \supset (Ba \cdot Bb) \ / (Aa \supset Ba) \cdot (Ab \supset Bb)$

Its truth table shows the premise true and the conclusion false:

$(Aa \cdot Ab) \supset (Ba \cdot Bb) \mathbin{/\!/} (Aa \supset Ba) \cdot (Ab \supset Bb)$
F F T 　T　 T F F 　　 F T T 　F　 T F F

(5) Let universe be *a*. Let Aa = F, Ba = T. The argument becomes

　　1. $Aa \supset Ba / Aa \equiv Ba$

Its truth table shows the premise true and the conclusion false:

$Aa \supset Ba \mathbin{/\!/} Aa \equiv Ba$
F 　T　 T 　　 F 　F　 T

8.6.I

1. $(x)(Px \supset \sim Txj)$

2. $(x)(Px \supset \sim Txx)$

3. $(x)[Px \supset (\exists y)(Py \cdot Lxy)]$

4. $(x)[Px \supset \sim(y)(Py \supset Lxy)]$

5. $(x)[Px \supset \sim(y)(Py \supset Lyx)]$

6. $(x)\{Px \supset (\exists y)[(Py \cdot Tyx) \cdot Lxy]\}$

7. $(\exists x)\{Px \cdot (y)[(Py \cdot Tyx) \supset Lxy]\}$

8. $(x)\{Px \supset (y)[(Py \cdot \sim Tyx) \supset \sim Lxy]\}$

9. $(x)\{Px \supset (\exists y)[(Py \cdot Tyx) \cdot \sim Lxy]\}$

10. $(x)\{Px \supset (y)[(Py \cdot \sim Tyx) \supset Lxy]\} \supset (x)(Px \supset Lxx)$

8.6.II

(1)

3.	$(x)Fxc$	2; EI
4.	Fxc	3; UI
5.	$(\exists y)Fxy$	4; EG
6.	$(x)(\exists y)Fxy$	5; UG
7.	$(x)Gxx$	1, 6; MP

(2)

2.	$(y)Fxy$	1; UI
3.	Fxx	2; UI
4.	$(\exists z)Fzz$	3; EG

(3)

2.	$(y)(Fxy \cdot Gyx)$	1; UI
3.	$Fxx \cdot Gxx$	2; UI
4.	$(z)(Fzz \cdot Gzz)$	3; UG

(4)

2.	$(\exists x)Fx$	ACP
3.	Fc	2; EI
4.	$Fc \supset (y)Gy$	1; UI
5.	$(y)Gy$	3, 4; MP
6.	Gc	5; UI
7.	$(\exists y)Gy$	6; EG
8.	$(\exists x)Fx \supset (\exists y)Gy$	2-7; CP

(5) 2. $(x)Fx$ 1; Simp
     3. $(y)Gy \cdot (x)(Fx)$ 1; Com
     4. $(y)Gy$ 3; Simp
     5. Fx 2; UI
     6. Gy 4; UI
     7. $Fx \cdot Gy$ 5, 6; Conj
     8. $(y)(Fx \cdot Gy)$ 7; UG
     9. $(x)(y)(Fx \cdot Gy)$ 8; UG

(6) 3. $(\exists y)Ixy$ 1; UI
     4. Ixa 3; EI
     5. $(y)(Ixy \supset \sim Mxy)$ 2; UI
     6. $Ixa \supset \sim Mxa$ 5; UI
     7. $\sim Mxa$ 4, 6; MP
     8. $(\exists y)\sim Mxy$ 7; EG
     9. $(x)(\exists y)\sim Mxy$ 8; UG

(7) In this example; the letters u, v, and w are used as variables, not as constants. In the text the convention is that they are constants. Deviation from the conventions of the text is employed here to make the proof easier to follow and to avoid complexities in instantiating.

| 3. $Buvw$ ACP
| 4. $(y)(z)[Buyz \supset (Luy \cdot Lyz)]$ 1; UI
| 5. $(z)[Buvz \supset (Luv \cdot Lvz)]$ 4; UI
| 6. $Buvw \supset (Luv \cdot Lvw)$ 5; UI
| 7. $Luv \cdot Lvw$ 3, 6; MP
| 8. Luv 7; Simp
| 9. $Lvw \cdot Luv$ 7; Com
| 10. Lvw 9; Simp
| 11. $(y)(Luy \supset \sim Iuy)$ 2; UI
| 12. $Luv \supset \sim Iuv$ 11; UI
| 13. $\sim Iuv$ 8, 12; MP
| 14. $(y)(Lvy \supset \sim Ivy)$ 2; UI
| 15. $Lvw \supset \sim Ivw$ 14; UI
| 16. $\sim Ivw$ 10, 15; MP
| 17. $\sim Iuv \cdot \sim Ivw$ 13, 16; Conj
| 18. $\sim(Iuv \vee \sim Ivw)$ 17; DM
     19. $Buvw \supset \sim(Iuv \vee Ivw)$ 3-18; CP
     20. $(z)[Buvz \supset \sim(Iuv \vee Ivz)]$ 19; UG
     21. $(y)(z)[Buyz \supset \sim(Iuy \vee Iyz)]$ 20; UG
     22. $(x)(y)(z)[Bxyz \supset \sim(Ixy \vee Iyz)]$ 21; UG

(8) 4. $(y)(z)[Bxyz \supset (Lxy \cdot Lyz)]$ 1; UI
     5. $(z)[Bxxz \supset (Lxx \cdot Lxz)]$ 4; UI
     6. $Bxxz \supset (Lxx \cdot Lxz)$ 5; UI
        7. $Bxxz$ AIP
        8. $Lxx \cdot Lxz$ 6, 7; MP
        9. Lxx 8; Simp
       10. Ixx 2; UI
       11. $(y)(Ixy \supset \sim Lxy)$ 3; UI
       12. $Ixx \supset \sim Lxx$ 11; UI
       13. $\sim Lxx$ 10, 12; MP
       14. $Lxx \cdot \sim Lxz$ 9, 13; Conj
     15. $\sim Bxxz$ 7-14; IP
     16. $(y) \sim Bxxy$ 15; UG
     17. $(x)(y) \sim Bxxy$ 16; UG

(9)   3. $\sim Ixy$ ACP
       4. $(y)[(Lxy \cdot Lyx) \supset Ixy]$ 2; UI
       5. $(Lxy \cdot Lyx) \supset Ixy$ 4; UI
       6. $\sim(Lxy \cdot Lyx)$ 3, 5; MT
       7. $\sim Lxy \lor \sim Lyx$ 6; DM
       8. $Lxy \supset \sim Lyx$ 7; Impl
          9. $\sim Lyx$ ACP
         10. $(y)(Lxy \lor Lyx)$ 1; UI
         11. $Lxy \lor Lyx$ 10; UI
         12. $Lyx \lor Lxy$ 11; Com
         13. Lxy 9, 12; DS
        14. $\sim Lyx \supset Lxy$ 9-13; CP
        15. $(Lxy \supset \sim Lyx) \cdot (\sim Lyx \supset Lxy)$ 8, 14; Conj
        16. $Lxy \equiv \sim Lyx$ 15; Equiv
       17. $\sim Ixy \supset (Lxy \equiv \sim Lyx)$ 3-16; CP
       18. $(y)[\sim Ixy \supset (Lxy \equiv \sim Lyx)]$ 17; UG
       19. $(x)(y)[\sim Ixy \supset (Lxy \equiv \sim Lyx)]$ 18; UG

(10)   3. $(\exists y) Lxy$ ACP
       4. Lxa 3; EI
       5. $(y)(Lxy \lor Lyx)$ 2; UI
       6. $Lxa \supset Lax$ 5; UI
       7. Laa 4, 6; MP
       8. $Lxa \cdot Lax$ 4, 7; Conj
       9. $(y)(z)[(Lxy \cdot Lyz) \supset Lxz]$ 1; UI
      10. $(z)[(Lxa \cdot Laz) \supset Lxz]$ 9; UI
      11. $(Lxa \cdot Lax) \supset Lxx$ 10; UI
      12. Lxx 8-11; MP
      13. $(\exists y) Lxy \supset Lxx$ 3-12; CP
      14. $(x)[(\exists y) Lxy \supset Lxx]$ 13; UG

167

(1) 3. $a = c$ 1, 2; Id
     4. $c = a$ 3; Id

(2) 2. $a = a$ Id
     3. $Fa \cdot a = a$ 1, 2; Conj
     4. $(\exists x)(Fx \cdot x = a)$ 3; EG

(3) 2. $x = x$ Id
     3. $(\exists y)x = y$ 2; EG
     4. $(x)(\exists y)x = y$ 3; UG
     5. Fa 1, 4; MP

(4) 2. $(x)(y)[(Fx \cdot Fy) \supset x = y]$ 1; Simp
     3. $(\exists x)Fx$ 1; Com, Simp
     4. Fa 3; EI
     5. $(y)[(Fa \cdot Fy) \supset a = y]$ 2; UI
     6. $(Fa \cdot Fy) \supset a = y$ 5; UI
     7. $Fa \supset (Fy \supset a = y)$ 6; Exp
     8. $Fy \supset a = y$ 4, 7; MP
     9. $(y)(Fy \supset a = y)$ 8; UG
    10. $Fa \cdot (y)(Fy \supset a = y)$ 4, 9; Conj
    11. $(\exists x)[Fx \cdot (y)(Fy \supset x = y)]$ 10; EG

(5) 2. $Fa \cdot (y)(Fy \supset a = y)$ 1; EI
     3. Fa 2; Simp
     4. $(\exists x)Fx$ 3; EG
     5. $(y)(Fy \supset a = y)$ 2; Com, Simp
     | 6. $Fx \cdot Fy$ ACP
     | 7. Fx 6; Simp
     | 8. Fy 6; Com, Simp
     | 9. $Fx \supset a = x$ 5; UI
     | 10. $Fy \supset a = y$ 5; UI
     | 11. $a = x$ 7, 9; MP
     | 12. $a = y$ 8, 10; MP
     | 13. $x = a$ 11; Com
     | 14. $x = y$ 12, 13; Id
    15. $(Fx \cdot Fy) \supset x = y$ 6-14; CP
    16. $(y)[(Fx \cdot Fy) \supset x = y]$ 15; UG
    17. $(x)(y)[(Fx \cdot Fy) \supset x = y]$ 16; UG
    18. $(x)(y)[(Fx \cdot Fy) \supset x = y] \cdot (\exists x)Fx$ 4, 17; Conj

CHAPTER 9

9.2

1. Direct method of agreement.

2. Inverse method of agreement.

3. Method of difference.

4. Method of concomitant variation.

5. Double method of agreement.

9.3

1. $1 - 1/13 = 12/13$

2. $1/52$

3. $(13 + 4 - 1)/52 = 16/52 = 4/13$

4. $(1/52)/(1/4) = 4/52 = 1/13$

5. $[(52 - 16)/52]/[(52 - 13)/52] = 36/39 = 12/13$

6. $12/52 = 3/13$

7. $6/36 = 1/6$

8. $2/36 = 1/18$

9. $2/6 = 1/3$

10. $3/5$

9.4

1. Unclear base for the percentage.

2. Sample, being all ministers, is biased. It does not fairly represent the general population.

3. Dispersion is ignored.

4. Characteristic attributed is not independent of the desires and purposes of those doing the attributing.

5. The meaning of average is not specified. Only if the *mode* is 19.6 years would this be a valid argument. Otherwise, some measure of the mean and the dispersion would be required to justify this conclusion.